HOLISTIC
ENERGY
MAGIC

Tess Whitehurst is an intuitive counselor, energy worker, feng shui consultant, and speaker. She has appeared on the Bravo TV show *Flipping Out*, and her writing has been featured in such places as the AOL welcome page, Llewellyn's annuals, and the *Whole Life Times* blog. To learn about her workshops, writings, and appearances, and to sign up for her free monthly newsletter, visit her online:

WWW.TESSWHITEHURST.COM

HOLISTIC
ENERGY
MAGIC

Charms & Techniques
for Creating a
Magical Life

WITHDRAWN

TESS
WHITEHURST

Llewellyn Publications
WOODBURY, MINNESOTA

FIRST EDITION
First Printing, 2015

Book design and edit by Rebecca Zins
Cover and interior photo: iStockphoto.com/34225022/©rvika
Cover design by Lisa Novak
Interior mudra illustrations by Wen Hsu
Interior ornament from the Art 1 India Vijay font

Llewellyn Publications is a registered trademark
of Llewellyn Worldwide Ltd.

Library of Congress Cataloging-in-Publication Data
Whitehurst, Tess, 1977–
  Holistic energy magic : charms and techniques for creating a magical life / Tess Whitehurst.—FIRST EDITION.
    pages cm
  Includes bibliographical references and index.
  ISBN 978-0-7387-4537-4
  1. Magic. 2. Force and energy—Miscellanea. I. Title.
  BF1611.W65 2015
  133.4′3—dc23

                                                              2014048977

Llewellyn Worldwide Ltd. does not participate in, endorse, or have any authority or responsibility concerning private business transactions between our authors and the public.
  All mail addressed to the author is forwarded, but the publisher cannot, unless specifically instructed by the author, give out an address or phone number.
  Any Internet references contained in this work are current at publication time, but the publisher cannot guarantee that a specific location will continue to be maintained. Please refer to the publisher's website for links to authors' websites and other sources.

Llewellyn Publications
A Division of Llewellyn Worldwide Ltd.
2143 Wooddale Drive
Woodbury, MN 55125-2989

www.llewellyn.com

Printed in the United States of America

Contents

CONTENTS

CONTENTS

PART 2:
The Holistic Energy Magic Spellbook   157

Introduction

For me, choosing what to write about all comes down to Joseph Campbell's famous bit of advice to "follow your bliss." In this case, as a longtime student and practitioner of energy work and the magical arts, I discovered a blissful hankering to deepen my metaphysical repertoire in certain ways. I was inspired to get in the habit of a daily elemental attunement meditation and to assemble an invisible toolbox of well-practiced bits of visualization and spellwork that could be whipped out anytime, anyplace, for any purpose, with zero physical tools or ingredients. I felt like honing and clarifying the more internal and energetic aspects of my magical practice.

Why was this such a blissful idea to me? Perhaps my favorite thing about living the magical life is the sense of personal power it bestows. Acting on the wisdom that you are essentially a pattern of energy that is inextricably interwoven with every other pattern of energy—including trees, the sky, other humans and animals, planets, rocks, and every other single thing that exists—you begin to truly feel and know that you are an important and beloved aspect of holistic oneness. Becoming conscious of the vibrations within and around you, and learning to shape and channel them according to your will, you begin to attune your life to the frequency of your truest and most authentic desires. All of this, as you might imagine or know firsthand, feels amazingly wonderful. Yes, challenges still arise, but seen in the context of meaningful interconnection and divinely fueled personal power, they feel less like the end of the world and more like the beginning of a fascinating new level of understanding.

After living this way for some time, you begin to know in an experiential way that the power on which you draw for your magical and metaphysical practices is not contained in external ingredients such as crystals, oracle cards, or herbs (although these things are great), but rather in you: it's all about your clear intention and belief in your success. What's more, because you are interwoven with all other patterns of energy, if you're familiar with them, you can call on them whether or not they are physically present in your space. Beginning to put this understanding into practice through working what I call "holistic energy magic" feels incredibly liberating and fulfilling. This way, no matter where you are, what you're doing, or who you're with, you can perform a bona fide and discreet magical ritual or metaphysical act to create positive change according to your authentic desire.

Clearly, my bliss did not steer me wrong. Through working with the principles in this book (some of which were already in my repertoire, some of which weren't), I have discovered a renewed sense of inspiration and empowerment. I sincerely hope that you have a similar experience.

Thank you so much for taking this journey with me.

Love and blessings,

Tess

Part I

Holistic Energy Magic Foundations

1

Secrets to Your Success

You have everything you need—right at this very moment—to live a life you love and manifest the truest desires of your heart. Even though this might seem farfetched at first, if you look more deeply, you can feel it, can't you? On some level you've always known it's there: that deep wellspring of power that is both one with everything and residing at the very core of your being, just waiting to be tapped into and fully expressed.

Whether you've been working with magical and metaphysical principles for some time or you're brand-new to the path, you've come to the right book if you're interested in shifting, shaping, and sensing energy in order to live harmoniously and create the conditions you want with what is already within and around you: mind, body, spirit, earth, and cosmos.

I'll admit that I love a good crystal, deck of oracle cards, or blessed candle as much as the next girl. But after years and years of working with focal items like these in magical spells and manifestation rituals of all varieties, I've come to understand that while lovely and picturesque (and even helpful and inspiring), they are absolutely not essential to my magical success. What is essential? Inspired, clearly defined intention—backed by vibrant visualization, symbolic action, grateful expectation, and, of course, the deepest possible alignment with All That Is.

You'll notice that these essentials are not available for purchase at a store. Rather, as I alluded to earlier, the seeds of each of them are already present within and around you right at this very moment. That means that no matter where you are, regardless of whether or not you have access to physical resources or metaphysical tools of any kind, you can perform feats of magic that will magnetize and activate your heart's desires. (Talk about convenient, cost-effective, and eco-friendly!)

So—while we'll return to them again and again throughout the book—let's lay a little groundwork right now simply by taking a closer and more experiential look at each of the essentials mentioned above. If you're already familiar with the principles of magic and metaphysics, we may be revisiting old territory. But because this territory is so vital to your magical success, it definitely bears revisiting. Just as gymnasts who can do double backflips still begin their floor workouts with the lowly cartwheel, even the most expert magical practitioners can benefit from reviewing the basics now and again.

While I'll initially present these essentials as separate entities, the truth is that once you get the hang of them, they'll usually manifest as an inextricable mishmash of two, three, four, or all five at once. (This sounds trickier than it is just because I'm breaking it down in order to explain it.) You'll really start to see what I mean a little later on in the book when you begin to put all this groundwork into practice. But for now, let's just look at the individual components so that you can begin to understand how they work and how to make them work for you.

Inspired, Clearly Defined Intention

Let's start with the first adjective: inspired. In order to manifest a particular intention, that intention must be inspired. In other words, it must be alive for you with passion, excitement, and joy. You can't just pluck an intention out of thin air, not really care that much about it one way or the other, and effectively manifest it. I'm not saying you can't take actions to force an uninspired intention into form, but the kind of manifestation we're talking about—the kind that is fueled by your passionate co-creation with the realm of Spirit and the realm of pure potentiality—simply does not apply to uninspired or inauthentic intentions.

Similarly, you can't authentically manifest something that someone else thinks you should want or that your ego—rather than your true self, the part of you that is one with the Divine and All That Is—wants. (Don't worry: chapter 2 is all about making sure that you're in the closest possible

9

alignment with the Divine, and therefore also with your truest and most authentic desires.)

Webster's says that inspiration is "a divine influence or action on a person believed to qualify him or her to receive and communicate sacred revelation" or "the act of drawing air into the lungs." An inspired intention would be one that—when you simply think about it and tune into it—elevates you to a feeling of being aligned with the realm of spirit, as if the intention itself uplifts and invigorates your consciousness with divine oxygen. That's because that breath of divine oxygen and alignment with spirit is the wind that will fill your sails and allow you to glide surely and steadily into the shining waters of your fondest desires.

"But," you might be wondering, "what about parking spots (and other seemingly uninspiring intentions)?" Well, consider that your life is one unified pattern of energy within the infinite pattern of energy that is eternity and the Universe. Within this unified pattern of energy, even the little things matter—including parking spots. That's why, if you wanted to manifest a parking spot, you would want to tune into the inspiration and joy behind the impending manifestation of this desire. For example, as you imagine easily and effortlessly pulling into a perfect spot, you might tune into the accompanying feeling of joy and the abiding knowledge that you are completely supported by the Universe in even the tiniest of ways. Acknowledging this inspired joy as you conjure the strong feeling that you've already pulled into your divinely designed spot (before you've actually done so in the physical world), you might heartily thank the Universe for this attentive and loving support by saying or thinking, "Thank you for my perfect parking spot!" By bringing this chosen future into your present-moment consciousness, you bridge the gap between what you desire and what is. This makes it highly likely that it will flow into your life experience.

As for the "clearly defined" part, you'll of course want to begin by knowing exactly what it is you want to manifest. For example, if you wanted to manifest a new job, you could just say, "I want to manifest a new job." And that's fine, but it's kind of open-ended, don't you think? With an intention like that, who knows what kind of job you might end up with? On the other hand, you don't want the intention to be so laser-focused that you leave the Universe out of the loop. For example, an intention like "I want to manifest a new job at the Such-and-Such Boutique" might seem really great from your finite human perspective, while the universal perspective (the part of you that is one with All That Is) may potentially have way, way better options in its line of sight.

That's why an ideally defined intention would be one that is very clear but not super specific, so that you might wind up with a job at Such-and-Such Boutique, but you also might wind up with something unexpected that turns out to be even better. So, staying with this example, we might choose this intention:

I want to manifest a new job that I love, that pays at least
$____, that is close to home, that allows me to only work
with respectful people whom I love and respect and who
love and respect me, that is in alignment with my values,
and that is surprisingly perfect for me in every way.

Once I've realized and stated my intention, I've found that it's ideal to rephrase it so that I'm stating it as if it's already true:

I now obtain a new job that I love, that pays at least $____,
that is close to home, that allows me to be surrounded
by respectful people whom I love and respect and who
love and respect me, that is in alignment with my values,
and that is surprisingly perfect for me in every way.

Alternatively, if you want to leave even more of the details up to the Universe, an intention can be phrased in a very short and to-the-point way while still being clearly defined. For example:

I now obtain a new job that I love and that is
overwhelmingly perfect for me in every way.

And if you really, truly, and undeniably feel fixated on a job at Such-and-Such Boutique and you just can't seem to get it out of your head, another alternative would be to say:

I now obtain a new job at Such-and-Such Boutique
or something even better and more ideal happens.

That way, you can state what it is that you think you want while leaving an opening for the Universe to work out something even better on your behalf.

Basically, just take your time and find a clearly defined intention that states exactly what you'd most like to manifest while resonating with power and filling you with a sense of exhilaration. Also make sure that it doesn't limit your potential for success in an undesirable way. Then phrase it in the present tense, as if it's already true.

Let's practice. Right now, choose at least one intention— one thing that you would like to manifest in your life. Phrase it according to the instructions above. Make sure that it's very clear but not overly specific. Also make sure that it's something that feels wonderful to you: something that makes your heart sing with real, honest-to-goodness joy. Phrase it in the present tense, as if it's already true.

HELPFUL HINT: Words That Open Doors

When phrasing intentions and affirmations, there are certain words and phrases that can create doorways of opportunity in your mind. By adding an element of surprise or conjuring up a freeing image—such as a road opening or obstacles vanishing—they help activate conditions that are even better than you initially could have imagined. This can be especially helpful when you feel that you could benefit from a boost of positive expectation and want to elevate your capacity to believe in a beautiful outcome. Here are some examples:

*I now expect the unexpected and receive wonderful
new financial opportunities in abundance.*

*We now discover and move into a new home that
is astonishingly perfect for us in every way.*

Happy surprises and unforeseen gifts are around every corner.

*I am astounded and overwhelmed by my abundant
wealth and amazing good fortune.*

*All obstacles vanish from my pathway, and beautiful
conditions flow into my life experience in abundance.*

*Ideal conditions are now fully activated in my life, and
I step into my most prosperous and auspicious flow.*

*Doors open everywhere. At every turn I instantly
recognize and immediately accept perfect opportunities.*

*I now experience unforeseen blessings
beyond my fondest imaginings!*

Vibrant Visualization

Once you've got your intention defined—whether it's as
heavy as finding a life partner or as light as finding a parking space—you'll want to fuel this intention with a vibrant
visualization of your imminent success. It's like in the first
Septimus Heap book, *Magyk*, when the ExtraOrdinary Wiz-

ard says, "And as you say the words you have to imagine the spell actually happening—that's the really important part."

There are many ways to go about visualizing. Some of them involve conjuring actual inner visions (such as an inner picture of the car that you'd like to have) and others involve conjuring feelings (such as the physical and emotional feeling of cuddling with a beloved soul mate on a lazy Sunday morning). Additionally, some visualizations are literal (like a vision of shaking hands with a new employer), some are symbolic (like a beautifully glowing golden key to your new home), and some are energetic (like a sphere of protective white light completely encompassing you and keeping you safe from harm). There can also be visualizations that are not visual at all. (I know it's a misnomer, but that's just the word that's sort of stuck in magical and metaphysical circles.) For example, some people are much more tactile than visual, so they might be more likely to conjure up the feeling of something in their hands or against their skin. Scents can also be a sort of visualization, as can sounds and tastes.

In my classes and workshops, as well as from reader emails that I've received, I've found that many people tense up around the concept of visualization. In much the same way that people claim they are terrible artists (incidentally, something I believe is never true; everyone is an artist), I've had people claim that they have trouble visualizing. If you are one of these people, please believe me: you're a great visualizer. Have you ever had a craving for something—a chocolate bar, for example? Did you want a bar of chocolate so badly that you could taste it? That's visualizing. Have you ever been so tired that you couldn't wait to curl up in your bed? That desire and accompanying inner picture or feeling is visualizing. Truly, if you couldn't visualize, you wouldn't be able to find your house on the street or your car in a parking lot. Your inner pictures (or feelings or senses) of these things are what allow you to recognize them. Even just deciding to stand up and walk across the room involves visualizing: before you do it, you set the clear intention to do so, and then you tell your body what to do based on what you have learned in the past, which manifests as pictures and feelings in your mind. Believe me: you're a great visualizer! No problem at all there. It's just a matter of recognizing when you're visualizing and then beginning to channel that talent—*which you have already mastered*—toward the manifestation of the conditions that you desire.

Something else to keep in mind while visualizing is that it's best to do it from a feeling place rather than a thinking one. In other words, approach it less like you approach a math problem on an aptitude test and more like you approach a dance floor at a wild party. Throw caution to the wind! It might feel a bit awkward at first, but if you stick to it and don't beat yourself up if you're not instantly "perfect" at it (whatever *that* is), you'll find that it won't be long before you're carried along in the natural flow of the moment.

To illustrate, and to begin getting you in touch with your unique style of visualizing, let's do a simple exercise now. Close your eyes and visualize (or imagine or feel) a very bright, blindingly bright little sunshine at your heart center: the center of your sternum. Feel it getting brighter, warmer, and more intense, and see or feel it beginning to pulsate with energy. Notice whether it feels more powerful for you to see this sunshine in your mind's eye or to feel it with your body (or both). Now hold your arms straight out to your sides, and send this light and energy from your heart center down your arms and out through the palms of your hands. Place your hands on your lower belly and send loving, healing energy to your digestive system and possibly (depending on your gender) your womb area. Notice that your heart light is infinite and is not diminished when you send light through your hands into another part of your body. Feel your lower belly bathing in this warm, healing light. Now, if there's any other part of your body that could use a bit of healing, place your hands there and direct healing energy into this area as well.

Symbolic Action

Symbolic action—something you actually do (like performing a gesture or assuming a posture) or say (like a mantra, affirmation, chant, or spoken charm) in the physical world— is arguably the least necessary of all of these essentials, although it can be an extremely effective way to unite your inner visions and intentions with a tangible action in the physical world. This has a number of benefits when it comes to successful manifestation.

- Symbolic action demonstrates your clear intention to your subconscious, thereby subtly yet powerfully aligning your future actions with your goal and tuning yourself to the frequency of your desires.

- Symbolic action demonstrates your clear intention to the Universe, thereby activating all forms of help from the unseen realm.

- Symbolic action helps shape energy according to your intention. This is a key aspect of magic and manifestation, as we are each a unique energetic pattern that interacts with all other energetic patterns as well as the grand web of energy of which we are all a part. This means that we are empowered to create positive change on an energetic level—both within and outside ourselves—if we so desire.

Practice time! Remember that intention that you so painstakingly phrased according to the previous instructions? Let's begin by taking the symbolic action of stating that intention three times out loud. Or, if you're in a public place or otherwise surrounded by people, you can write it three times. Either way, do so with great belief and conviction. Don't just mutter it or scribble it as if you couldn't care less. Say it or write it proudly and with utter certainty. As you do so, feel pure power and potentiality flow through your voice (or pen) and out into the world. If you're alone, you can even sing your intention, or yell it, or dance while you sing it! (Feel free to do this more than three times if you want to play with possibility.) Can you feel how taking the intention into the physical realm through speaking or writing it gives it extra juice? Can you feel the inner alignment with the compass of this desire?

Let's try another really simple symbolic action. Choose an emotion or quality that you'd like to feel a little (or a lot) more of in your life: confidence, self-love, romance, or financial prosperity, for example. Now hold your body as if this quality is currently present in your life in abundance. If you're alone, you can stand up and walk around. If you're not feeling totally free to do something like this right now because of the situation you're in, just subtly change your posture and facial expression where you're sitting. How would you hold your shoulders if you felt a huge upwelling of this emotion or quality? Would you slump or would you stand with your spine straight and your heart open? How would you walk? How would your face look? Conjure up this emotion or quality simply through your body's posture. Stay with this for at least a minute or two, then notice what a difference it makes in your inner environment.

Grateful Expectation

During and after your manifestation efforts, you'll want to be filled with a calm sense of grateful expectation for your forthcoming success. This is a vital aspect of the manifestation process, and believe it or not, it's also an area that causes a lot of confusion for some people. So let's take a good look at the subtleties of this essential.

Imagine that you're at your friend's house, and that friend just happens to be an expert on tea. She asks if you would like some tea. "Yes," you say, "I would love some. Thank you." And you really mean it. Even though your friend's tea is always different and you never know exactly what to expect, one thing you do know is that you always love it and that it's somehow always exactly perfect for the mood you're in at any given time. In fact, you can't imagine anything you would like more at this very moment than a cup of tea in the expert and intuitive way that your friend prepares it. You notice how grateful you feel as you rest in the utter certainty that a cup of this lovely tea is on its way to you now.

This is the quality of grateful expectation that is most beneficial to the manifestation process. You are utterly certain that you will receive something wonderful, even if you don't know precisely the form it will take. Why do you feel this way? Because, like your friend the tea expert, the Universe is utterly trustworthy in this regard. You also feel this way because you've tuned your intention to the exact frequency of your desire in a way that is clear but not specific. By letting go and trusting—remembering your intention but letting go of all urgency and attachment surrounding it— you allow all your efforts to be released into the divine web of manifestation in a way that is most conducive to success.

Notice that when you're experiencing this quality of grateful expectation, you're not desperately running into your friend's kitchen and watching everything she does in order to micromanage her. You're also not obsessing on the rapidity with which the tea arrives; you're enjoying the moment and allowing it to come to you in its own time and in its own way. You're joyfully expecting something wonderful to flow into your life experience in a way that is both light and easy.

So grateful expectation involves both a release and an embrace simultaneously. You release worry, obsession, and attachment to the form that your manifestation will take. You embrace joy, gratitude, and the feeling that something wonderful is about to happen.

To practice this feeling of grateful expectation, you could go to your favorite restaurant when you're really hungry and order a meal that you love. (Or if you want to practice your visualization technique at the same time, you can just visualize doing so.) As you're happily and gratefully waiting for the meal, notice the quality of your expectation: it's not too serious or heavy, but at the same time it's utterly certain. It's excited but not obsessive. Now that you're familiar with it, you can conjure this feeling again during and after your magical workings in order to help bring about the best possible outcome and highest possible degree of success.

The Deepest Possible Alignment with the Divine

At the very core of working successful magic in a holistic way is cultivating and maintaining a very deep alignment with the Divine. Now, I know that the concept of divinity is a loaded one that means different things to different people. For our purposes, let's think of it as All That Is: the harmonious unified field and the part of you that is one with everything. In fact, all of you is one with everything because all is one. But you might say that this current life experience is characterized by the illusion of separation. While we are all, in fact, part of one single sea of energy, it appears that we are separate individual beings. If it didn't appear that way, we would be so interwoven with cosmic consciousness that we wouldn't know our own names, have any concept of time, or recognize our hometown. What we are doing when we work magic and play with manifestation principles is drawing upon the truth (that we are one with everything) in order to affect the illusion (the individual components of our seemingly separate, seemingly finite life experience).

You might think of this life experience like pure sunlight shining through drops of moisture in the air to create a rainbow. Is the light actually red, orange, yellow, green, blue, indigo, and violet? No. It's white. But because of the temporary illusion of separation, we get to glimpse the variation and gradation of white's subtle components. Because of this same illusion of separation, artists get to endlessly play with these colors when they create their masterpieces. And that's exactly what we, as magical practitioners, are also doing when we play within the illusion of separation in order to create beauty in our lives and in the world.

In addition to creating positive change in individual (and ultimately illusory) life areas, when we align ourselves with the Divine to the best of our ability, an added benefit—and perhaps the best of all benefits—is that we feel a sense of grounded serenity at the core of our being. While challenges may come and go, at our center we realize that we come from infinity and return to infinity. There is truly nothing more inspiring, liberating, or more conducive to joy.

But how do we really, deeply align with the Divine and stay in alignment as a matter of course? As I mentioned, doing so is the regular, everyday work of the successful magical practitioner, and it's also the subject of the next chapter.

2

Elements in the Ether

Like an acorn or a sapling or a sprawling oak tree, your life possesses a natural ideal expression. Also like an acorn, sapling, or oak, this ideal expression will be most likely to come to its fullest fruition when the conditions are right: in essence, when you're connected to the world around you—earth, air, sunlight, water, and cosmos—in the most auspicious and nourishing of ways.

In this modern culture, where we are often removed from the habitat that was native to our species for the majority of the time our species has been present on this planet—i.e., the bare earth beneath our feet, fresh air in our lungs, sunshine on our face, and natural bodies of water rushing around our skin—it is easy to forget that *we* are aspects of nature and are inextricably interwoven into the web of life, just like any other living being. Forgetting a truth that is so vital to our well-being has vast repercussions that resonate throughout every aspect of our physical and emotional health. In effect, it effectively cuts off our magical and spiritual oxygen. We can start to not only feel disempowered, but also isolated, abandoned, and left out in the cold.

That's why communing with nature restores our emotional equilibrium and holistic magical power. If you will recall, I define the Divine—our spiritual lifeblood and the source of our magical power—as the oneness of all and our connection with All That Is. And nothing reminds us of our connection to All That Is like the natural world around us and glittering sky above us, on which we rely not only for our inspiration, but also for every single other thing we need in order to survive, such as food to eat, water to drink, and air to breathe.

Because it's our present intention to work energy magic—magic without physical tools—it's of particular importance that we cultivate a strong relationship with the Divine as it's represented in the physical world around us. This is because magic is a holistic spiritual practice that sees the solid, visible aspects of the world as inextricably interconnected with the ethereal, invisible aspects of the world. The eternal mirroring and interaction of the polarity of seen with unseen and of form with spirit is an invaluable point of power. Through nurturing a strong awareness of, and interconnection with, the physical world (as animated by God/Goddess/All That Is), we calibrate our inner equilibrium and drink deeply from the wellspring of magic that dwells in the place between the worlds.

In addition to spending time regularly in the great out-doors, we can fortify this awareness of our vital connection to the earth and cosmos by cultivating a conscious relation-ship with the five elements: earth, air, fire, water, and spirit. The more deeply we can align with these elements—daily, as a matter of course—the easier and more effective it will be when we work energy magic. This is because the ele-ments will be strong within us, reducing and even remov-ing the need for us to draw power and focus from physical ingredients.

Conscious alignment with the five elements has been one of the aims of magical and spiritual practitioners from diverse traditions and countries for thousands of years. While the five-element system we'll be talking about in this chapter is common to a number of western folk and Neo-pagan magical traditions, there is a similar system present in both Chinese alchemical practices (such as feng shui and acupuncture) and the Indian healing tradition known as Ayurveda; see the table on the following page. Clearly there is something instinctual and archetypal about this way of perceiving and interacting with the world around us, and clearly it works, otherwise these systems would not have survived and thrived from ancient times up until the pres-ent day.

WESTERN	CHINESE	AYURVEDIC
earth	earth	earth
air	wood	air
water	water	water
fire	fire	fire
spirit	metal	ether

Five-Element Parallels

With all of this in mind, let's take a good look at each of these elements: what they are, how we can align with them, and how we can employ them to establish balance and activate magical power. You might want to use these descriptions to take note of what elements you're already in harmony with, and also to notice what elements you could benefit from connecting with more fully.

At the conclusion of this chapter, we'll talk about regular habits that you can establish in order to internalize and metabolize these teachings so that they can become an inextricable component of your everyday consciousness. We'll also look at some magical actions that you can take anytime throughout the day to instantly align with a certain element or generally balance your elemental equilibrium.

While reading through the following descriptions, please keep in mind that because we interact with the elements in a holistic way, harmonious alignment with any one element is much more likely if you're in harmonious alignment with the other four elements. Please also note that just like Gold-ilocks and the porridge, we're looking for a happy medium: being out of sync with an element may entail being out of touch with it or overly attached to it (at the exclusion of one or more of the other elements).

Earth

In its most primordial sense, the earth element is the ground beneath us: what makes up the land on which we stand. It's also gently rolling hills, meadows, fields, forests, rocks, sand, mud, and clay. Although we're made up of all five elements in some regard, our physical bodies are very much repre-sentations of the earth element, as are the physical bodies of other land creatures and plants. The earth element also encompasses food and all physical items: basically, anything solid that you can touch.

When we're harmoniously connected to the earth ele-ment (not too attached and not too distant), we feel safe and nourished. We feel energized and relaxed—never anx-ious. Essentially, we're deeply grounded and feel at home in the world.

Walking barefoot outside, gardening, hugging a tree, or simply spending time in nature can deeply connect us with the earth element. But one can also connect with the earth element indoors in a number of ways, such as by:

* lying flat on the floor, on your belly or back

* noticing the weight of your body
   on the chair or floor

* touching your belly lovingly and becoming aware of your physical body

* conjuring up the scent of rich, wet earth

* imagining the feeling of lying on soil or soaking in a mud bath

* envisioning roots going deeply into the earth

* visualizing oneself hugging (or being) a tree

* eating a plant-based meal while consciously and gratefully connecting with the earthy origins of its ingredients (root vegetables and grains are especially helpful for this purpose)

Facing north can also support or strengthen the intention to connect with the earth element, as this is the cardinal point associated with it.

Air

Air, naturally, is the invisible stuff that surrounds us and sustains us; it's also the wind blowing through trees and canyons, and the breathable layers of our earthly atmosphere. Creatures that fly—birds, bats, butterflies, and dragonflies—are emissaries of the air element, and symbols of air include wings, feathers, clouds, and plants that the air loves to blow through, such as willows and palms. Because it's aligned with the east and new beginnings, the sunrise is also a potent symbol of this element.

When we're ideally aligned with the air element, we feel fresh and alive. Creativity flows to us and through us in a satisfying way, and we feel comfortable with the swift, mercurial realm of words and ideas. Inspiration is the way of things, so life never feels stuck or stale.

Listening to the wind in trees, watching clouds float across the sky, and feeling fresh air in our lungs can powerfully connect us with the air element. But one can also connect with the air element indoors in a number of ways, such as by:

- simply noticing your breath as it goes in and out of your lungs and feeling gratitude for this subtle yet essential and constant nourishment

- doing the yogic breath exercise known as "ujjayi breath" by sitting with your spine straight and closing your eyes. Begin to breathe loudly in a long and light way, letting the breath slightly catch in your throat in order to make a louder noise. When you feel ready, close your mouth and continue this aspirated breath, soothing yourself with the ocean- or wind-like sound of the air moving through your throat. Continue for up to five minutes.

- lighting a stick of incense and watching the smoke, realizing that it is air patterns made visible

- lighting a bundle of dried white or desert sage (so that it's smoking like incense) and smudging

yourself and your home with the smoke, being
very careful to catch any burning embers in a dish

* closing your eyes and envisioning wind
whipping around your body

* closing your eyes and envisioning yourself
soaring through the sky like a bird

* visualizing and inwardly communing with winged
fairies, birds, dragonflies, bats, and butterflies

Facing east can also support or strengthen the intention
to connect with the air element, as this is the cardinal point
associated with it.

Fire

In its physical representation, fire is the sun's vibrant flame
that bathes our earth in light and warmth. The fire element is also present in lava, forest fires, candlelight, electric
light, heaters, stoves, and the fires that we create and gather
around in our homes and outdoor spaces. In a holistic and
magical sense, it is passion, movement, aliveness, joy, laugh-
ter, social connections, performance, music, radiance, righ-
teous anger, and cleansing transmutation. Symbols associated the fire element include the phoenix, dragons, snakes,
lizards, fireworks, hibiscus blossoms, and candles.

When we're agreeably in tune with the fire element, we
feel passionate and alight with radiant excitement. We feel
that we can transform old, stuck energy and challenges into

positive energy, artistic fuel, and expansive movement. We take joy in connecting and sharing with others and do not shy away from expressing our feelings clearly and with love, even when this entails actively addressing things about which we feel angry or uncomfortable.

Feeling sunlight on our skin, gazing at sunlight as it twinkles in water and on fresh green leaves, and standing reverently or dancing wildly in front of a bonfire can activate the fire element within us. One can also connect with the fire element indoors in a number of ways, such as by:

- envisioning a very bright sun at your heart center, solar plexus chakra (between your belly button and heart), or in your lower belly. As you breathe in see this blinding sun get brighter and more intense, and as you breathe out see it expand. Continue this visualization until the sun completely fills your entire body and aura.

- envisioning a candle flame and consciously merging with its essence

- envisioning standing before a bright bonfire, hearing the sound of it crackling and feeling the warmth of it all along the front of your body

- envisioning standing inside a burning plain and becoming one with the fire. Feel yourself dancing and swaying like flame, and feel all negativity burning away and transmuting into light.

• doing the yogic breath exercise known as the "breath of fire." To do this, sit with your legs crossed, curl your fingers against your palms, and extend your thumbs. Extend your arms up over your head in a V with palms facing forward, thumbs pointing up. With your eyes closed, extend your tongue and begin to rapidly pant like a dog, thinking the mantra *sat nam* (which means something like "I am the embodiment of truth") with every breath in and out. When you feel ready, bring your tongue inside your mouth, close your lips, and continue this panting through your nose, still thinking the mantra *sat nam*. Continue for up to three minutes. (When done correctly, while this will fill you with an energy buzz, it should not make you feel like passing out. However, if you happen to feel dizzy or overly lightheaded, stop immediately.)

Facing south can also support or strengthen the intention to connect with the fire element, as this is the cardinal point associated with it.

Water

Obviously, the water element appears in the natural world in rivers, lakes, streams, ponds, waterfalls, oceans, and rain, and it appears in our homes and outdoor spaces in the form of fountains, wells, swimming pools, and all plumbing features. Our bodies, while solid and sensory (and therefore associated with the earth element), are made up in large part (perhaps 70 percent) by this fluid, cleansing, quenching, and nourishing element. Water is also associated with emotion: like water, we say that emotions well up, overflow, or run deep. Similarly, we describe developing an emotional attachment as falling in love (like falling into a lake) or falling hard (like falling rain). We also, like waves, describe emotional peaks as things that overwhelm us or carry us away. As a physical example, when we cry, you might say that saltwater tears wash toxins associated with stagnant emotions out of our spirits and souls.

Symbols of the water element include fish and other aquatic animals, mermaids, wavy and asymmetrical shapes, and the moon (which is aligned with the ocean and the tides).

An aspect of attunement with the water element is an ability to be fluid in our ways and to allow things to organically flow along their natural course. When we are in balanced alignment with this element, we also let our emotions flow freely, connect with others and ourselves in an authentic way, listen to and follow our intuition, enjoy sensual and sinuous movement, and express ourselves artistically in ways that bring us joy.

Bathing in or spending time near a natural body of moving or pristine water can instantly align us with the water element, as can gazing at the moon and consciously connecting with its essence. Ways to connect with the water element indoors include:

- gazing at or listening to an indoor water feature

- taking a sea salt bath

- listening to New Age music featuring watery sounds

- visualizing swimming in or spending time near a beautiful body of water

- envisioning ocean waves engulfing you and cleansing your entire being. See the saltwater drawing out all impurities and refreshing you with a healthy dose of negative ions.

- envisioning energetic ocean waves moving through and cleansing your home

- blessing water and then drinking it consciously. For example, you might hold a glass of water in both hands and visualize rain falling into the ocean at midnight. Consider that, while temporarily separate, this water is both a representation of and an actual part of all water that exists everywhere. Give thanks for it, and then drink.

- becoming aware of the water within you that moisturizes and nourishes every part of your body

- dancing and moving as if you were a river or stream

Facing west can also support or strengthen the intention to connect with the water element, as this is the cardinal point associated with it.

Spirit

The spirit element is the most transcendent of the elements: it encompasses, animates, interweaves, and invisibly underlies all things, including the other elements. Additionally, it includes what lies outside of our atmosphere: space, our solar system (and all solar systems), our galaxy (and all galaxies), stars, black holes, and everything else out there in the outer (and inner) reaches. It is the music of the spheres and the structure of the cosmos: the sacred geometrical patterns and rhythms that govern and characterize everything we see and understand as well as everything we don't see and can't understand. Spirit is also that inexplicable and yet undeniable factor that gives us life and that continues after we die. It is sometimes known as the Great Mystery, God/Goddess, and All That Is.

Symbols of the spirit element include lightning bolts, spirals, circles, planets, stars, and sacred geometrical patterns such as fractals and mandalas. As emissaries of the heavenly realm, birds also symbolize the spirit element, as do angels, winged deities, and deities related to weather and the sky.

When the spirit element is ideally activated and present in our life, we don't feel overly disturbed by thoughts of mortality and the unknown; rather, we feel fascinated and even empowered by them because we clearly sense the eternal and omnipotent aspect that underlies the illusory appearance of death and separation. We see everything in terms of energy, which makes it possible for us to recognize the subtle patterns at work, in turn allowing us to shape our life conditions for the better and even avert potential challenges before they manifest into form. What's more, we understand how magic works in an experiential rather than theoretical way. This supports our intention to work magic consciously and wield it effectively.

Examining the night sky through a telescope or simply gazing at the stars can help align us with the spirit element. Contemplating and meditating on sacred geometrical patterns in nature—such as blossoms, concentric ripples across still water, spider webs, or a hummingbird's rhythmic choreography—can connect us with this element as well. Ways to connect with the spirit element indoors include:

- gazing at the sky out the window and attempting to contemplate its staggering size

- examining and contemplating the current placement of planets and constellations through a smartphone app such as Skyview

- studying astrology and noting the current aspects

- gazing at satellite photos of planets and outer space

- becoming conscious of weather patterns and predictions

- calling on angels

- finding a deity, pair of deities, or group of deities who inspire you and connect you with a sense of

the Divine and All That Is, and then honoring
them each day through devotional activities such
as chanting, praying, or invoking. And, like an
offering of fragrant smoke on an altar, you can
also devote your efforts (such as your career
efforts or daily chores—in essence, any energy
that you put out into the world) to these deities
as an affirmation of aligning yourself and your
actions with their divine energy. (To do this, you
would simply affirm that it is your intention to
do so, and then act with that intention in mind.)

• staying quiet for at least five minutes and
connecting with silence and open space. Because
we spend so much time doing things, saying
things, and filling our time with activities of
every variety, this can be a time of emptying
out and listening deeply so that spirit can enter
your life and you can be aligned not so much
with things but with the space in between.

• noticing the quiet stillness between this and that:
for example, while you're waiting in line, you could
rest in the pause and reach out your consciousness
to connect with the empty space of the cosmos. Or,
when you're listening to classical music, you could
revel in the sacred silences between the sounds.
Similarly, when you're listening to someone speak,

you could tune into the ineffable significance
of the quiet moments between the words.

- meditating on or gazing at sacred
  geometrical patterns

- coloring or drawing mandalas or other
  sacred geometrical patterns

Standing or sitting with your spine straight can also support or strengthen the intention to connect with the spirit
element, as this grounds you solidly on the earth while
opening the major pathway of energy in your body—which
lies along your spinal cord—to receive energy and information from the divine, heavenly realm through your crown
chakra, which is the energy center at the crown of your head.

HELPFUL HINT: Look to the Stars

Magical practitioners since time immemorial have diligently cultivated a working relationship with the dance of
the planets, the cycles of the earth, the path of the sun, and
the tides of the moon. All of these things have to do with
the spirit element: the element associated with space, the
cosmos, the interweaving of the other four elements, and
the sacred underlying patterns that animate and orchestrate
all things.

An earnest exploration of your personal astrological charts (both Western and Eastern) as well as a regular
monitoring of the astrological aspects at work can be an
invaluable method of coming into deeper attunement with

the elements. The benefits of astrological awareness are far reaching: in addition to tuning you to the frequency most beneficial to your magical success, it can also help you to recognize and harmonize with the patterns at work in your life, provide extremely useful insights into other people, and generally help you navigate and sail smoothly along the energetic tides of life.

There are countless books available on the subject of astrology, and I highly suggest poking around and finding the ones that most interest you. That being said, I have found that some great references to have on hand include *The Only Astrology Book You'll Ever Need* by Joanne Martine Woolfolk, *The Handbook of Chinese Horoscopes* by Theodora Lau and Laura Lau, and *Llewellyn's Astrological Calendar* (an annual publication). I also like taking a peek at my smartphone apps: Skyview (to see where the planets and constellations are on any given day) and Deluxe Moon Basic (to see what's going on with the moon).

Everyday Alignment and Calibration

As I mentioned at the beginning of the chapter, in order to work effective magic without any physical ingredients or tools, it's especially important for us to take time to align with the five elements every day (or almost every day). It's also important that we continually strive to deepen this alignment throughout our lifetime and that we learn to consciously calibrate our elemental balance as needed.

The Elemental Altar

Most magical practitioners enjoy having an altar in order to fortify their spiritual consciousness with inspiring symbols in the physical world, often with symbols of the five elements as primary focal points. If you haven't already done this, although this book centers on energy magic rather than magic with many physical components (and even *because* of this), I highly recommend that you bring such an altar into your personal space. This one physical magical act will serve as a daily reminder of your alignment with the five elements, thereby increasing your ability to draw upon them in a non-physical way.

To do this, find or obtain a small table or other flat surface (such as a shelf or the top of a bookcase) that feels right for your altar. Next, select one symbol for each of the five elements. Here are some ideas for what you might choose (although please do not feel limited by them):

EARTH
- a rock

- a small, healthy living plant in soil

- a ceramic dish

- a dish of salt

- a dish of soil

AIR

- an incense holder with incense (this can be an especially useful symbol to choose, as it can double as a way to offer incense to the Divine, aka the spirit element)

- a naturally shed feather or feathers

- a bundle of dried white or desert sage

- a handheld fan

- a chain of tinkling bells

FIRE

- a candle (this can be an especially useful symbol to choose, as it can double as a way to bring life to your altar and signify spiritual communion)

- an essential oil burner

- volcanic rock

- a small sun- or star-shaped sculpture or figure

- an attractive lighter or matches

WATER

- a seashell

- a small goblet or bowl

- a small bottle or jar of rainwater

- a river rock

- beach glass

SPIRIT
- a symbol or statue of a deity, deities, or group of
  deities with whom you feel particularly connected

- a symbol or statue of an angel or angels

- a symbol or statue of a bird or birds

- an image of our galaxy or solar system

- a spiral image

- a sacred geometrical image or sculpture

Because spirit is an all-encompassing element, place your chosen spirit symbol in a central location and arrange the other four symbols attractively around or in front of it. If possible, make a note of the cardinal directions associated with each of the four earthly (non-spirit) elements, and place the symbols accordingly. (If you don't have a compass lying around, smartphones usually have a compass feature.) You may prefer to forgo the directional orientation in order to arrange them in a way that feels right to you.

Daily Work

For serious magical practitioners, it's absolutely necessary to engage in daily alignment work. (Or *almost* daily. I personally prefer adding the word "almost" so that I remember that I'm striving for consistency rather than perfection.) Busy magical folk will be relieved to know that—provided that you do indeed commit to doing the work just about every day—even five to ten minutes can do the trick.

Over time, your practices will shift and change as you discover what works best for you, and it's also a good idea to change your practices as necessary in order to keep your inspiration fresh and alive. Still, below you'll find a simple starting point for daily alignment work. (I personally find that where magic is concerned, simple is always best.) Of course, feel free to adapt this in whatever way feels right to you.

SIMPLE DAILY ALIGNMENT PRACTICE

Choose a regular time that works best for you (such as first thing in the morning, as soon as you get home from work, or last thing before you get ready for bed). Make sure that you will not be disturbed for at least five to ten minutes. Perhaps light a candle on your altar, as well as a stick or cone of incense.

Face north, perhaps holding your earth symbol in your hands, and close your eyes. Conjure up the scent of fresh soil, the image of a fertile field at night, and the feeling of cool dirt beneath your bare feet. Say, "Earth, I call on you." (Set down the earth symbol if you've been holding it.)

Face east. With your eyes closed, and perhaps with your air symbol in your hands, envision the sound of wind in trees, the image of a sunrise, and the feeling of fresh breeze caressing your skin and blowing through your hair. Say, "Air, I call on you." (Set down air symbol.)

Face south. With your eyes closed, and perhaps with your fire symbol in your hands, envision the sound of crackling flames, the image of a bonfire or the blinding sun, and the feeling of a fire or sunlight warming your skin. Say, "Fire, I call on you." (Set down fire symbol.)

Face west. With your eyes closed, and perhaps with your water symbol in your hands, envision the sound of rushing water or waves crashing, the image of the ocean or a bubbling stream enveloping you, and the feeling of water against your skin. Say, "Water, I call on you." (Set down water symbol.)

Now face north again. Raise your arms above your head, palms open to the sky. Tilt your head slightly upward. Envision yourself with roots going deep into the earth and branches reaching high into the cosmos. Feel yourself draw nourishing golden light up from Mother Earth and inspiring clear light with rainbow sparkles down from Father Sky. Envision the molten core of the earth below and the infinite swirling cosmos above. Say, "Spirit, I call on you."

Place your hands at your heart and feel the five elemental energies that you have summoned all present within your heart. Say, "I am balanced, I am aligned, I am whole. I am one with the earth, the sky, the cosmos, and All That Is." Depending on how much time you have, you can now visualize, imagine, and affirm anything you'd like to experience in the upcoming day and in your life in general. You can also take a moment to shield and protect yourself, your home, and your loved ones with visualized spheres of light.

When this feels complete, to thank the elements face west and say, "Water, I thank you." Face south and say, "Fire, I thank you." Face east and say, "Air, I thank you." Face north and say, "Earth, I thank you." Still facing north, connect with earth and sky as you angle your arms upward and say, "Spirit, I thank you." Place your hands on your heart again and say, "Thank you, thank you, thank you. Blessed be. And so it is."

Finally, to stabilize yourself and to realign in your newly calibrated state with the physical world around you, place your hands on the floor or lie flat on your back, visualizing any excess energy that you may have raised draining deeply into the earth (even if you're on the second floor or higher). Strongly connect with your gravitational relationship with the solid floor and your energetic relationship with the earth.

Weekly Work

In addition to your daily alignment work, you'll want to make sure that you're connecting with the natural world at least once a week. This might be through gardening, spending time gazing at the stars, sitting around a fire pit, taking a run in your neighborhood park, or going for a hike in the woods. If weather does not permit this weekly communion, indoor options for connecting with the Divine through the actual elements themselves include:

• gazing out the window and consciously
  connecting with the earth and sky

• connecting with the natural world around you
  during your indoor meditation. For example,
  I like to think of the way the earth might have
  looked in my neighborhood before it was paved
  and populated by humans, and to lovingly
  acknowledge its raw natural beauty in this imagined
  state. (I find that the earth remembers!)

• paying special attention to your houseplants.
  Connect with their spirits and recognize
  their soil as an indoor emissary of
  the primordial earth element.

• taking a sea salt bath and recognizing it as an
  actual representative of the water element and
  an incarnation of the ocean's vast depths

• stepping outside for a brief second, but wasting
  no time in acknowledging and connecting
  with the elements as you see them (just
  as you would lovingly connect with an old
  friend even during a brief encounter)

• burning a fire in your fireplace or lighting a bunch
  of candles on a plate to connect with warmth,
  the fire element, and the spirit of the sun

Activators

Finally, when you're out in the world or desire to instantly strike up a deeper connection with one or more elements without using any physical tools, you can employ these elemental activation practices. The more you practice them, the easier and more like second nature they will become. You might want to start with them exactly as they're written and then adapt them according to what feels most powerful for you.

EARTH ACTIVATOR

If you're feeling frazzled, anxious, or otherwise ungrounded, it could be time to activate your connection with the earth element. To do so, place your right hand on your lower belly and your left hand on your heart. As you conjure up the scent of wet earth, patchouli, or sweet white blossoms (such as jasmine, honeysuckle, tuberose, gardenia, or neroli), bring to mind the feeling of lying belly-down on cool, wet earth. Feel cradled and nourished as you release any excess tension or fear into the heart of the earth for composting. Notice your breath as it goes in and out, and feel your weight on the earth. Feel solid and safe. Inwardly thank the earth element.

AIR ACTIVATOR

If you're craving freshness, quickness of thought, creativity, and a sense of new beginnings, you might activate your connection with the air element. With your elbows against your sides, angle your forearms up and out to the sides. With palms facing out, touch your thumbs and little fingers. Close your eyes and envision/imagine/feel a fresh breeze whipping around you as you gaze at the newly rising sun. Pucker your lips and inhale deeply, then exhale deeply with your lips still puckered; repeat three times. Feel energized and alive. Inwardly thank the air element.

FIRE ACTIVATOR

For passion, movement, enthusiasm, and powerful transformation, consider activating your connection the fire element. Close your eyes and visualize a blindingly bright, golden red-orange flame burning at the center of your navel. See it expand outward until it fills and radiates from your entire body and aura. With your elbows against your ribs, forearms angling out, and palms facing out, flick your fingers forcefully outward as you pant through your nose. (See previous "breath of fire" exercise.) Every time you exhale, flick your fingers. Every time you inhale, bring them back to tuck under your thumbs. Repeat for up to one minute. Then, breathing normally, visualize the ball of fire getting smaller and smaller while still retaining its brightness and potency. See it eventually becoming the size of a silver dollar and dwelling just beneath your navel. Place your hands there and feel the subtle and balanced effects of the fire element moving throughout your body and consciousness. Inwardly thank the fire element.

WATER ACTIVATOR

For cleansing, emotional healing, activating the intuition, and releasing rigidity in favor of fluidity and flow, activate the water element. Standing upright, relax your body so that your knees are soft and your arms are hanging at your sides. Feel that you are grounded in the ocean floor while lightly floating vertically in cool ocean water, like a tall seaweed frond dancing in the current. Release tension in your neck and let your head and body rock gently and loosely from side to side. Feel cool water rush around you as you visualize the slow rhythm of this underwater landscape. Release attachment to outcome and metaphorically allow yourself to be cleansed and gently buffeted about by the flow. Inwardly thank the water element.

SPIRIT ACTIVATOR

To connect with space consciousness, to bring yourself into the present moment, to activate your intuition and personal power, and to witness the magical and miraculous in all things, activate the spirit element. Forming your arms into one long diagonal line, point your right arm at the sky and your left arm at the earth, index fingers extended. (This is like the Magician card in many tarot decks.) Allowing your consciousness to follow the direction of your right hand, connect with the glittering, spiraling, infinite cosmos above. Allowing your consciousness to follow the direction of your left hand, connect with the deep, creative, receptive, mysterious womb of the earth. Now bring the energetic awareness of each to meet at your heart, throat, and third eye. Feel aligned with the space between things and marvel at the mystery of the moment. Inwardly thank the spirit element.

3

Your Invisible Magical Toolbox

I adore the idea of an invisible magical toolbox. In addition to being filled with priceless and endlessly useful treasures, an invisible magical toolbox can go everywhere with you— without raising any eyebrows, cluttering up any rooms, or requiring you to check any baggage. Not to mention, unlike a visible toolbox, it's not actually separate from you. Once you cultivate a relationship with the exercises in this chapter, their energy will become an aspect of your personal energy and their power will become an aspect of your personal power. It's sort of like enhancing the usefulness of your computer or smartphone by downloading apps or upgrading the operating system.

While this entire book is fundamentally about stocking and developing your invisible magical toolbox, this chapter gets the momentum going by starting you out with some especially useful essentials.

You might start with these exactly as they're written or adapt them according to what feels most powerful for you. You might also find that as you work with them over the next few months or years, and even over the course of your life, they'll shift and evolve. This is natural, as every magical practitioner is different and everyone is always changing. Additionally, because it's ideal to keep your magic fresh and inspiring throughout your lifetime, if you find yourself getting into a rut at any point, it might be time to clear out, adjust, or restock your invisible magical toolbox.

The more you practice with these tools, the stronger and more substantial they will grow within you. As you read through and get acquainted with each tool, you can practice conjuring it up and putting it to work. After that, you might like to set aside time to practice doing this one or two times per week or you can seamlessly merge your practice time into your day by employing them as the opportunities naturally arise. In time, utilizing these tools will become like second nature, just like making tea or riding a bike.

But before we go any further, let's make sure we're on the same page with the whole "free will" thing.

Caveat: Energetic Magic and Free Will

Because we're about to get into some actual magical techniques that are likely to in some way affect the lives of people other than you, it's important for us to take a moment to discuss permission and free will. If you're an experienced magical practitioner, you already know that it's generally considered unethical to perform magic on behalf of another—or plain old *on* another—without express permission from the person themselves. I find that there are some exceptions to this rule, as well as some slight differences when working magic that is purely performed in the energetic realm without any physical tools.

For example, in cases where I want to perform energetic magic for the express purpose of healing or supporting another in a way that I know they will benefit from, I find that it's just fine to obtain the needed permission by having a conversation in the nonphysical realm. In other words, where purely positive, nonspecific energetic magic is concerned (such as sending healing or supportive energy or love), I might simply tune into the other person's spirit, whether they're physically present in the room with me or not. Once I feel that I am sufficiently connected, I might ask them (in my visioning mind, not with my actual voice) if it's okay for me to perform magical energy work on their behalf. If I get an inner okay, then I'll proceed. This might come in the form of a vision of them nodding or smiling, an auditory sense of them saying yes, or just a strong emotional feeling of affirmation. If I don't receive an inner okay, I won't.

And if I want to perform a supportive, nonspecific form of magic (such as healing or protection) on behalf of people or animals who have already trusted in me to help them (this would include beings such as companion animals, children, convalescing parents, and friends who have confided in me), I would just go ahead and work the magic, taking their physical-world trust as confirmation of their nonphysical-world trust.

Now, this would simply not fly if we're talking about performing magic *on* someone rather than *on behalf* of them. For example, you *cannot* tune into someone's energy and then ask them, "Is it okay if I perform a spell on you to make you fall in love with me?" or "Is it okay if I perform an energetic ritual with the intention of getting you fired?" This is because if you're even considering working magic like this, you are clearly biased and can't be trusted to receive an accurate answer. Additionally, for intentions like this it will be of much greater benefit for you to concentrate purely on what you'd like to experience (such as romance or harmony at work) rather than focusing on how you can manipulate others according to what you *think* will help you experience what you want to experience.

This also would not fly if we're talking about creating specific conditions for another that we are not totally sure that they desire or will benefit from, which would also fall under the category of manipulation. For example, if you decide that you want to work magic on behalf of your adult daughter so that she will have a baby, though she has not recently expressed the desire to have kids (even if you think you know that she will love it), I would definitely not recommend trusting yourself to ask her on the energetic plane if it's okay for you to do so.

Just to be clear: it's a good idea to get permission in the physical world unless we're talking about one of the following (in which case it would be okay for you to ask on the energetic plane):

- a divine, unspecific intention such as love, healing, cleansing, protection, or emotional support

- something that the person has expressly asked you for support about (such as healing or manifesting a new home)

And finally, of course, it's my belief that you don't have to ask at all if you're performing magic that has to do with self-defense, provided you're only sending out purely positive (or neutral) nonspecific energy, such as protective light or transmuting flame.

Now that we're all clear, in the words of Willy Wonka, "Yes? Good! On with the show."

The Cauldron of Lilac Fire

The cauldron of lilac fire is a tool of transmutation. In other words, it's a tool that cleanses away negativity by transforming it into positivity and blessings. It draws upon a vibrant lilac-colored (pink-violet) light that is a dynamic combination of cool, receptive, blue lunar light and bright, active, red solar light. Together, these colored lights form a lilac-colored fire that can naturally balance and powerfully purify pretty much anything you'd like, including (but not limited to) people, objects, relationships, physical spaces, and situations.

Once you really get to know the lilac fire and it's strongly present within your inner landscape, you can call on it by itself and mentally direct it into and around things, beings, and situations without even closing your eyes, and we'll talk about how to do that shortly. First, though—and regularly throughout your life (in order to refresh and revitalize your connection with it)—you'll want to inwardly acquaint yourself with its origins and see it in all its blazing glory.

Here's a visualization that will help you do just that. As with most extended visualizations, begin by relaxing comfortably, with your spine straight, in a place where you won't be disturbed.

CAULDRON OF LILAC FIRE VISUALIZATION

It's a dark night outside in a meadow, and the stars are bright. You're standing in the center of a large sacred circle. Although you cannot see the beings that make up the outer circle with your physical eyes, you know that they are there and sense their presence at this magical site. They are the wise ones from times past. They are the primordial ancestors and the sacred spirits of nature.

At the very center of this circle is a giant silver cauldron filled with extremely dry leaves, sticks, and logs. To your left, on one side of the cauldron, is the Moon Goddess; robed in blue, she glows with an ethereal and iridescent light. To your right, on the other side of the cauldron, is the Sun God: robed in red, he blazes with a golden-red fire. The deities gaze at each other over the cauldron with bright eyes of love. Holding their palms toward the cauldron, they ignite a bright lilac fire within it that immediately flares upward toward the stars.

As you hear the lilac fire crackling, you sense and know that it will rage on forever. You can feel a searing power emanating from it, and you know beyond all doubt that whatever is placed within it shall be powerfully cleansed, purified, and harmonized. It has the unique power to ignite stuck or frozen energy and transform it into light, warmth, and movement. The fire has an inner wisdom that knows what is not needed and how to shift it into precisely what will be of value. It transforms challenges into blessings, confusion into confidence, and roadblocks into open paths.

The Moon Goddess and Sun God look at you, and you sense that they want you to go into the flames. With perfect love and perfect trust, you inwardly agree to this and instantly feel yourself being swiftly lifted and placed within the fire. You allow the crackling lilac flames to move through you and around you, thawing out what is frozen, burning away what is old and dead, shining light into the darkness, and transforming all into positivity, energy, and heat.

When this feels complete, you find yourself standing outside of the flames once again while they continue to rage on eternally. Inwardly, you thank the Moon Goddess, Sun God, circle of wise ones, earth, sky, and lilac fire.

In addition to placing yourself inside the cauldron during this visualization, you can place other people or companion animals within it, or even objects (such as crystals or charms) that you'd like to be cleansed and activated.

As I mentioned above, the more you do this visualization, the stronger the lilac fire will become within you and the more you'll be able to wield it easily and efficiently throughout the day. When you feel ready to try this, you might simply call on the lilac fire itself and visualize it filling and surrounding your body, your home, your car, or your workplace. If you find yourself dealing with a challenging situation or a situation that feels stuck, you can conjure up a sense of the situation—with all of its tension and struggle, and perhaps any pictures or areas that you associate with it—and then send the lilac fire into it from every angle. If you're in the situation currently, you can send it into and around the area and everyone involved in the situation. You can also employ the lilac fire if you want to energetically cleanse an item in a pinch (such as a secondhand art piece or a library book).

If it feels helpful, you could choose a word, sound, or hand gesture that aligns you with the lilac fire. For example, every time you call upon the violet fire (starting with the visualization exercise), you might angle your right forearm up, palm facing you, and touch your pinky to your thumb to symbolize the cauldron, letting your middle three fingers symbolize the flames. Additionally, the number three can symbolize the two forces—lunar and solar—that become one. This way, you will strongly associate the gesture with the visualization, which will help you to call it up more swiftly and with greater clarity.

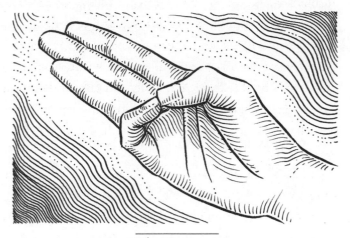

Lilac Fire Gesture

Finger as Wand

Many magical practitioners work with wands made of any number of natural materials, such as crystal, metal, or wood. Most often these are used as tools of focused projection (such as projecting healing energy into a person or directing protective energy into a charm) or focused absorption (such as absorbing cosmic energy from the heavens or receiving healing energy from a crystal).

While wands can be great fun and hold a unique magical energy all their own, the fact of the matter is that index fingers can work just as well, if not better, than external wands and fulfill all the same purposes.

Every magical practitioner is different, so you'll want to experiment, practice, and find what works best for you. Let's start with some general guidelines to get you started, and then we'll move onto some exercises you can employ for practical purposes or simply practice to help you hone your expertise.

General Finger-as-Wand Guidelines

- Consider that magical power generally flows through your body along a vertical path: when standing this means it flows from your feet to the top of your head, and when sitting this means it flows from your tailbone to the top of your head. Conversely, just as it flows from earth to heaven along your spinal cord, it also moves from heaven to earth. You might also imagine this energetic path moving down into the earth like the roots of a tree (and drawing energy up) and moving upward into the sky like branches (and drawing energy down).

- To direct energy through our arms and hands, we employ energy centers (some call them chakras) that are located along the central thoroughfare of our spinal cord in order to direct it outward rather than along its usual vertical path.

- While the energy center in the middle of your forehead (third eye chakra) focuses the intention and visualizes the path that the energy will take, the energy center in the middle of your sternum (heart center) is the roundabout

where the energy pools just before it moves
down the arm and out through the hand.

• To employ a finger as a wand, choose the index
finger that feels the most powerful for the purpose;
for most of us, this will be our dominant hand.
Then, with your arm straight, point your finger so
that it is in one long, straight line with the rest of
your arm. This will ensure that the energy flows
most freely and abundantly from your heart center.

• Now, using your mind to focus your intention and
being sure that you are consciously connected to
earth energy and the energy of the cosmos (ideally
by having recently performed your simple daily
alignment practice from the last chapter), feel
energy pool at your heart center, then consciously
allow it to flow out through your finger.

• For many people, the index finger of the non-
dominant hand will be most effective for receiving
and absorbing energy. To practice absorbing
energy, point your finger at the sky while angling
your palm up, as if you are beckoning to the sky.
Now, using the energy center at your forehead to
visualize the path you intend for the energy to take,
use the receptive energy at your heart center (the
energy that yearns and pines for people that you
miss or that causes you to desire to hug someone

deeply to your chest) to draw some of this cosmic light down and into the center of your heart. You might feel yourself drawing this energy down as you inhale, and then visualize it pooling at your heart center as you exhale. Once you feel yourself receive a noticeable amount of this energy, point your finger down at the ground and project the energy into the earth in order to ensure that you aren't overly energized or ungrounded. (This will have the added benefit of giving the earth a burst of neutral energy that can be used for healing.)

Finger-as-Wand Exercises

CAST A CIRCLE

In an area where you have enough floor space to cast a circle around yourself that's about four to five feet in diameter, stand facing north and connect with the element of earth (see previous chapter). Then fact east and connect with the element of air. Turn to face south and connect with the element of fire. Face west and connect with the element of water. Once again, face north, and now connect with the element of spirit. Point the index finger of your dominant hand (or whichever finger you prefer to use for projective exercises) down at the northern point of the circle you wish to cast. Visualize/imagine/feel the bright white or clear light of the cosmos and the golden-white light of the earth merging at your heart center and moving down through your arm and out through the tip of your finger. Like a golden

laser beam of blinding light, see it moving from your finger-
tip and out to the ground. Steadily, and at a moderate pace,
rotate in a clockwise circle as you draw a circle of light on
the ground around you. In your mind's eye, see the circle
glowing. (If necessary, start slower and build up to a more
moderate pace.)

You are now contained within a protective and energetically nourishing circle of light. If you like, you can sit down
or remain standing and work any additional magic or manifestation exercises that you desire; being within the circle
will give them an extra dose of focus and power.

Before you leave the circle, you'll want to open it.

OPEN A CIRCLE

To open a circle that you've cast using your finger as a
wand, face west and thank the element of water. Face south
and thank the element of fire. Face east and thank the element of air. Face north and thank the element of earth. Still
facing north, now thank the element of spirit. Now, twirl or
spin counterclockwise in one full 360-degree circle. At the
completion of the spin, raise your arms up over your head
and then release them outward, as if you're throwing petals
to the sky.

After opening a circle, it's a good idea to earth any excess
power that you may have raised.

EARTH POWER

To earth power after opening a circle or anytime you'd
like to draw off excess energy and return to a healthy, everyday energetic set point, point both index fingers down

toward the ground, arms straight in front of you and angled 45 degrees away from your body, palms down. Visualize any excess energy within you and around you moving down your arms and out through your fingers as you send it down into the core of the earth. Finish by kneeling or sitting down, placing your palms flat on the floor. Use this gesture to consciously connect with the physical, earthly realm.

EMPOWER AN ITEM, FOOD, OR BEVERAGE

To imbue and infuse a certain item (such as a crystal, a piece of jewelry, or an article of clothing), food, or beverage with a particular quality of magical energy, begin by connecting to the spirit element, becoming aware of your weight on the ground as you send roots deep down into the earth. Then become aware of the crown of your head growing branches and connecting with the glittering cosmos above. Feel the earth and spirit energy mingling and mixing within your body and aura before intensely pooling at your heart center.

Once you feel connected with and nourished by this infinite power source, conjure up the quality you'd like to infuse within the item, food, or beverage, and allow it to shift the vibration of the universal energy within you in a way that feels powerful and significant for you. For example, if you wanted to infuse something with the energy of healing, you might feel a cool, fresh, minty rush of energy at your heart. Or, if you wanted to infuse it with the energy of self-love, you might feel a deep upwelling of love toward yourself as you inwardly see golden and pink sparkles move throughout the energy at your heart.

When you feel ready, point your finger at what you would like to empower and send this energy down your arm and out through your finger into it. In your mind's eye, see it swirling and pulsating with this energy. When this feels like it has reached a natural peak, bring your hand back down to your side, once again connect with the energy flowing in through your feet and head, and then earth the power (as in the previous section).

You can then eat or drink the item to internalize the magic or keep the item nearby as needed. You can also give the item to someone else to eat or drink, or to keep nearby, provided that they have willingly and knowingly accepted your magical assistance.

The Emerald Heart of Healing

The emerald heart of healing is a powerful energetic healing method that you can perform on behalf of any sentient being, whether or not that being is in physical proximity to you. Here's how to do it:

If the person to whom you'd like to send healing energy is in the room with you, ask her to sit comfortably in front of you so that you are facing one another, perhaps three to five feet apart. Alternatively, she can rest in a reclining chair or on her back on a bed. (In this case, you'll want to stand in front of her in such way that you can easily direct your palms toward her heart center.) If the person is not in the room with you, close your eyes and visualize this person sitting or reclining in front of you, and keep your eyes closed for the remainder of the exercise. Sitting or standing with your spine straight and your feet flat on the floor, connect with your infinite power source: feel energy coming up from the core of the earth and down from the infinite cosmos and meeting at your heart center.

Now visualize/imagine/feel your heart center swirling with a clear, clean, blinding emerald light. Know this light to be a radiation and representation of omniscient healing wisdom: it brings exactly what is needed to bolster immunity, soothe pain, increase vitality, and strengthen one's ability to heal. With straight arms, now direct your palms toward the other person's heart center (or visualized heart center). As you inhale, feel the healing light getting brighter and more potent within you. As you exhale, send it out through your palms and directly into the other person's heart. Stay with this until it reaches a peak. Then move your arms down and reconnect with the energy of the earth and sky. Finish by earthing the power.

Palms of Power

The palms of power technique allows you to infuse any person, animal, or object (including yourself and any part of your body) with positive energy of any variety. By now, I imagine you're starting to get the gist of the way energy flows throughout your body and aura, as well as how you might consciously direct it for any number of magical intentions. As in the previous exercises, before wielding the palms of power you'll want to connect with the abundant power of the earth and the infinite power of the cosmos.

Once you've brought these energies to meet at your heart, take a moment to tune the energy to the frequency of your intention. For example, you might want to choose the energy of pure love, in which case you might conjure up the scent of roses and an inner vision of pure white or pink light while feeling as much love as you possibly can. Or, if you want to choose the energy of relaxation, you might conjure up the sound of gentle ocean waves, the scent of coconut, and an inner vision of cool blue light.

Once you've tuned the energy, cup your hands gently with your fingers side by side, as if you're wearing mittens. Then, as you send energy through the center of your palms, direct your palms toward what you would like to empower, holding them just a short distance (two to four inches or so) away from the object or being. If possible, you might cup or sandwich the object between your palms so that you're directing energy inward from two opposing angles.

The Mirrored Sphere

The mirrored sphere is part protective bubble, part ninja invisibility cloak. As a resident of a big city, I find it invaluable for times when I need an extra dose of protection, as well as times when I would prefer not to be looked at (e.g., when I feel a creepy stare pointed in my direction).

Plus it's really simple: all you do is visualize a huge mirrored sphere around yourself, instantly reflecting any and all energies pointed your way right back to where they came from. This way, if a person is directing envy, unwelcome lust, or any other undesired thoughtform your way, it will bounce right off of you and go right back to its source. And if someone is leering at you or simply making you uncomfortable or self-conscious, they will no longer see *you* but rather will see some sort of reflection of themselves. On really sunny days, they might also be sort of energetically blinded, causing them to avert their eyes.

Elements as Tools

The more familiar you get with the five elements, the more easily you can employ them as magical tools. Here are some ideas for how you might do this.

Earth as Grounding Tool

If you feel frazzled, anxious, or generally ungrounded, you might call upon the element of earth by envisioning yourself buried in moist, rich, fertile soil, like a seed. Know that you can easily breathe under the earth, and feel her cool, relaxing, centering, cradling energy on your skin and all throughout your inner organs and extremities.

Earth as Cleansing Tool

To cleanse yourself, a loved one, your home, or any physical space, you can imagine the earth beneath you or the area (even if it's a number of floors down). Now feel the earth drawing out discord and negativity, like a clay mask draws impurities out of your skin. Feel the earth receiving the challenging energies with love and with the absolute ability to compost them into nourishing positivity.

Air as Clarity-Enhancing Tool

To refresh and bring clarity to your mind or to any situation, call on the element of air. Then envision yourself standing on a hilltop at sunrise as wind whips around you, caressing your skin and blowing through your hair.

Air as Cleansing Tool

To cleanse yourself, your home, or any physical space with the element of air, call on the element of air and then envision clean wind whipping around you or through your space, blowing away and dispersing any stuck energy or negativity.

Fire as Protection Tool

There is a traditional magical protective oil known as "fiery wall of protection." Similarly—and without any oil at all—you can envision an actual fiery wall of protection keeping negativity of all forms strongly at bay. Simply call on the element of fire, visualize a fiery wall, and place it around yourself, your home, or any person or area that you'd like to protect.

Fire as Cleansing Tool

To employ fire as a cleansing tool, simply call on the element of fire. Envision fire filling and surrounding what you'd like to cleanse, powerfully burning away any and all stuck or negative energy and transforming it into heat, light, and positivity.

Water as Healing Tool

Just as tears are our body's natural way of washing away emotional pain, you can call upon the element of water to soothe and heal emotional or physical pain. To do so, call on water and envision/imagine/feel a wave washing over and around you, completely drenching and immersing you in the cool ocean tides. Calling to mind the way that water smoothes rocks and breaks down mountains into sand, feel it smoothing painful edges and powerfully dismantling the energy behind physical or emotional ailments.

Water as Cleansing Tool

To cleanse yourself, a loved one, or a physical space, you can just call on water and see ocean waves rushing in, around, and through what you'd like to be cleansed. See the saltwater absorbing and neutralizing negativity as it power-fully disinfects and purifies everything in its wake.

4

Your Energetic Palette

Just as visual artists use things like paint, pencils, canvas, and clay to bring their inner visions to life, magical practitioners employ energetic qualities to help manifest their intentions, enhance their life experiences, and shape their lives. This is why, when we work magic with physical items, we might employ a crystal or a few leaves of a certain herb or a cloth in a particular color—not because we need the item in order for our magic to succeed, but because we desire to swirl one or more of its energetic qualities into the mix. As always, our clear intention is the only necessary ingredient, but the presence of the item can help serve as a reminder of the quality that we're conjuring up and a focal point for our unbending concentration. And because in magic we see everything as alive, with its own spirit and unique energy, we can draw magical power from the item's living spirit that bolsters our intention and colors our creative manifestation.

See, but the thing about the physical world is that it's really not as physical as it seems. From a scientific perspective, it's definitely not solid: everything is energy. Even a huge mountain or a mass-produced plastic toy is completely composed of, and alive with, vibrating energy. Additionally, the spirits of things, such as flowers, herbs, or crystals, are not localized, and—because we are, in truth, one with everything—they are not separate from our own beings. In other words, we can call upon the spirit of fresh roses and potently bring their energy into our magic without actually having a single rose in the room.

While it can require a bit more practice and expertise, you may find that magic drawing on nonphysical ingredients and energies can, in many ways, be more potent than magic employing physical ingredients. Perhaps this is because nonphysical magic requires one to have a deep personal relationship with the ingredient, until it's essentially an aspect of one's own personal energy field. At that point, the ingredient can be employed in a more intense and fantastical way. For example, while the red rose in a love spell can smell sweet and look gorgeous, I find that conjuring up the clear inner vision of a whirlwind of intensely fragrant red rose petals or simply calling upon the abiding spirit of all red roses everywhere can have a much quicker, more pervasive, and more intoxicating effect.

As you walk along your spiritual and magical path, you'll discover that you have an affinity for certain ingredients that can be employed in a nonphysical way—such as inner visions of colors, scents, plants, and crystals—and you'll naturally desire to nurture and enhance this affinity through communing with these ingredients in both the physical and nonphysical realms. While each of us interacts with each energetic essence in our own unique way, this chapter will acquaint you with some of the many useful magical ingredients that you can swirl into your palette (in addition to the elements, which we've already discussed). The more you practice with them and cultivate a relationship with them, the more powerful and successful your magical workings will become.

Please be aware that your relationships with these ingredients will be different than my relationships with them, and also that your relationships with them will shift and change throughout your lifetime. This is normal and even ideal because we're all different and we're always changing. Being awake and alert to these differences and changes means that the state of our personal energy is healthy and vital. It means that we're moving with the current of our lives—growing, moving, expanding, and adapting—rather than feeling limited or staying stuck in the past.

Color and Light

As we've seen, visualized color and light can be valuable magical tools. As with all the ingredients described in this chapter, you can use them alone or as a base containing other energetic items or visuals such as scents, patterns, items, or sounds.

Perhaps the most basic color or light exercise would be to visualize a sphere of a color or light of your choice completely filling, surrounding, and encompassing you. (For this exercise I sometimes like to call upon an image of the blinding brilliance of the sun, even if I'm visualizing a color other than golden-white. I find that this vision can be easily adapted to portray any color I choose.) You can also visualize a color or light coming up from the core of the earth and entering your feet and tailbone, then moving up through your body like a bubbling flow of energy. Similarly, you can visualize a color or light coming down from the cosmos, entering the crown of your head, and then swirling down through your body like a colored liquid merging and mixing with a clear one. Other patterns to play with include waves, spirals, champagne bubbles, whitewater bubbles, fountains, bonfires, or sparkles.

Colors and lights can also be projected through your palms or fingertips (as in the palms of power and finger as wand exercises) into other people, objects, areas, or even into parts of your own body.

Below you'll find some guidelines for working with these colors and lights, but please do not feel limited by them. If, for example, when considering a particular magical intention you feel strongly drawn toward a particular color—even if the intention doesn't appear in the color's description below—this would be highly significant. As always, trust your intuition and let your natural sense of expansiveness and joy fuel your magical momentum.

Black

Like a vision of deep water or deep earth, the color black can help us return to the vast inner power and authenticity that resides at our depths. It is extremely absorbent and neutralizing, and it helps when excessive or ungrounded energy is present. It's also associated with poetic consciousness, mystery, the otherworld, and feminine power; in Taoist alchemy (for example, in the yin-yang symbol), black is aligned with the feminine, or receptive, principle. Visualized black light or the color black can be protective by absorbing negativity, but it will eventually get saturated with it, so you might not want to surround yourself in a sphere of blackness or black light if you're surrounded by negative energy. Rather, you might call upon the color black to neutralize anxiety or frenetic energy, or to absorb any negativity within you. (For the latter intention, you'll want to then replace it with something to transmute such as golden-white light or violet flame.)

Light Blue

Like a clean stream or a bright sky, light blue can bring feelings of freshness, clarity, energy, and joy. Because it's so clean and positive, and because like attracts like, it can also bestow a sense of peaceful protection. Additionally, it facilitates effective and harmonious communication. I find that it pairs well with the scent of mint, sparkles, or the sound of a bubbling stream.

Royal Blue

Royal blue is perhaps my favorite protective color. In fact, I often like to surround myself with a very bright sphere of protective royal blue light before I leave the house. (Actually, I call on archangel Michael to do so for me—we'll talk more about him in the next chapter.) In a way that I can't explain or fathom, this leaves me feeling comprehensively impermeable to negativity. Royal blue can also be a very peaceful and energizing color, and one that helps align us with the joyful, healing aspects of the water element.

Brown

Brown light and the color brown can help heal, balance, and harmonize us through tapping us into the power of the earth. It can be useful for magical intentions such as grounding, sensuality, and emotional stability. Magical practitioners particularly aligned with the earth element might draw upon brown light in order to recharge their magical batteries.

Brown with Golden Flecks

Bright brown light with golden flecks (reminiscent of tiny mirrors in sunlight) can be a very powerfully protective energy in which to surround yourself or your loved ones, especially if grounding is an issue. When I lived on the second floor in a city apartment, and since I feel particularly aligned with the earth element, I found this light to be very useful for increasing feelings of harmony, balance, nourishment, stillness, and stability.

Clear with Rainbow Flecks

A vibrant clear light with tiny rainbow flecks can be an excellent way to visualize and conjure the universal, cosmic light of infinity and pure potentiality. You can also summon it or surround yourself with it to increase creativity and cheer and to awaken to the magic of life.

Emerald Green

Emerald green is traditionally associated with the heart chakra (the energy center located in the middle of your sternum), and it corresponds with love, health, healing, renewal, vitality, and wealth. It's especially helpful for healing heartbreak and grief, for increasing self-love and the belief that one deserves to prosper, and for bolstering the body's ability to heal itself. When working with emerald green light, it can be useful to remember that it possesses perfect healing wisdom in and of itself. In other words, there is no need to micromanage *how* the light works or what changes it actually brings about. It's more useful to recognize the light as innately wise, and to let go and trust that it will bring exactly the shifts that are most needed at any given time.

Forest Green

Forest green light—in addition to its alignment with health, healing, and prosperity—facilitates grounding and fosters harmonious connections within families and groups.

Mint Green

Like light blue, mint green has a fresh, clarifying, uplifting energy. When healing, clarity, energy, or vitality are needed, mint green can be a good color to choose for protection and general positivity.

Grey

Grey is the ultimate color of neutrality. When you desire to detach from your emotions, step out of conflict, rise above discord, or act without attachment to outcome, grey is an excellent color to choose. Grey's ability to help establish neutrality can be useful before choosing to work magic for any purpose, especially when the topic of our magic contains a strong emotional charge for us. For those who are prone to extremes, grey also can help establish a healthier balance and moderation.

Indigo

In the chakra system, indigo is associated with the third eye (the energy center in the middle of your forehead) and intuition, inner vision, and clear knowing. As a shield, it can be powerfully protective. The purple aspect transmutes negativity into blessings as the blue aspect provides an armor against any additional negativity.

Lavender

This soft violet light can bring beauty, balance, and a heightened expectation of magic and miracles. It possesses a benign receptivity that can infuse one's presence with a tastefully subtle (yet very real) magnetism. It also has a gentle transmuting quality, which means that it turns negativity into positivity and blessings. For all these reasons, it can be a good color or light to choose when desiring to increase attractiveness or prosperity consciousness.

Lilac

As discussed in the previous chapter, lilac (a bright pinkish purple) can be employed for powerful transmutation, especially when visualized as a vibrant burning fire.

Orange

Orange is associated with the harvest and the sacral chakra, which is located at the lower belly and reproductive organs. It can be visualized in this area of the body for sexual healing, healing the sexual organs, fertility and potency, and help with digestion.

Peach

Like a ripe peach on a summer day, this color is warm, fuzzy, and sweet. It encourages warm relations between partners and groups, facilitates loving communication, and helps establish an affable quality of peace. It's an extremely social color, and its bright positivity also makes it helpful as a color of protection. It can be great for romance as well, as it's a well-rounded balance of sweetness, grounding, and passion.

Pale Pink

Pale pink, like cotton candy, is soft, comforting, and sweet. It can be helpful for heart healing and for increasing feelings of self-love and self-acceptance. Its comforting and soothing vibrations also make it a good choice when working with children.

Warm Pink

Warm pink is also extremely soothing. It relieves stress by helping us get out of our heads and into our bodies, and it can be a useful color to work with to bring tranquility and facilitate restful sleep. My brother and I once surrounded ourselves in warm pink light before a particularly challenging social event that we felt compelled to attend, and we found that it effectively softened the edges and kept us cocooned in bubbles of positivity. It was especially lovely that the warm pink light succeeded in doing this without creating any harsh energetic disturbances or undesirable repercussions. We coasted through the event as if we were wearing rose-colored glasses and wrapped in warm fuzziness.

Red

Red is the color associated with the root chakra (the energy center at the tailbone), and it connects us powerfully with our physicality and the earth. As the color of blood, it's also been traditionally associated with health, vitality, passion, life force, fire, and feminine power in a large number of ancient cultures across the globe. For all these reasons, it's the color that was most associated with magic and protection throughout the ancient world. As a resident of a frenetic, warm, and sunny city, I don't find myself calling on red light very often, but I can imagine doing so if I lived in a sleepier, colder, or cloudier area in order to bring balance by filling myself or my living space with active, fiery life force energy. Do be careful, however, as red is also the color of anger and addiction, and it can create greater discord if these energies are already present. To be safe, I would only call on red light sparingly or when you feel like there is an excessive water imbalance—in other words, when you feel as if you are drowning in depression, sadness, or grief, or if there is a lot of this type of emotion energetically lingering in an interior space.

Teal

The immune chakra—located at the thymus (halfway between the heart and throat chakras)—is associated with the color teal. Envisioning this chakra as filled with teal-colored light (or directing light toward this area with a finger or the palms), then envisioning this light expanding to fill the entire body and aura, can be an excellent visualization to support physical healing for oneself or another. (This might be considered as an alternative to the emerald heart of healing exercise, especially if you're doing preventative healing work.) The thymus is also associated with clearing old energetic patterns, so after bringing to mind a pattern that you'd like to clear and setting the intention to clear it, you might try lightly tapping the thymus with your fingertips while visualizing yourself encompassed in teal light. Continue for up to one minute.

Violet

Violet is the color of the crown chakra (the energy center at the top of the head) and is associated with spirituality and connection with All That Is. Because of this, it can help open our eyes to our magical consciousness and awareness of the otherworld—the realm of the unseen and eternal. Violet's primary colors of red and blue are both associated with wealth and luxury in their own ways (through fiery success and abundantly flowing water, respectively). This, coupled with the fact that violet dye was at one time extremely rare and expensive, makes violet a color of great wealth, prosperity, and luxury.

Bright White

Bright white light is highly purifying and protective. Because it reflects all colors, it can be employed as a powerful shield from all forms of negativity. By envisioning bright white light filling and surrounding your entire body and aura, you can also activate stuck energy, remove emotional and spiritual toxins, and dissolve challenging thoughtforms in the bright light of awareness. In interior spaces it can dissuade the presence of earthbound spirits by ushering them into the light or at least shifting the vibration to one that is less tolerable to them. It can also simply clear the space and generally activate and elevate the vibe.

Golden-White

Reminiscent of sunlight, golden-white light possesses similar properties to simple bright white light, although it's coupled with a warmer, earthier, more grounded aspect. This makes it a good all-purpose light to call on for general protection, purification, healing, and activation.

Yellow

Yellow is associated with the solar plexus chakra (located about halfway between the bellybutton and the heart center), as well as its accompanying aspects of personal power and control. When a feeling of anxiety or lack of empowerment is present, it might be beneficial to breathe into the solar plexus area, envisioning a small sunshiny sphere of very bright yellow light residing at this energy center. As you breathe in, you might draw earth energy up through your root and see it activate and empower this little yellow sun. As you breathe out, you might see this chakra spin faster, spinning off any negativity or debris, which then immediately dissipates and disperses. As you continue to do this, the yellow gets clearer and the chakra becomes more and more perfectly sized: not too big and not too small. Continue until the chakra feels and looks perfectly clear and balanced to your inner eye.

Crystals

If you have a magical relationship with a crystal, you can call upon its energy even when it's not physically present to receive similar benefits and channel its power toward manifesting what you desire. For example, you might send the vibration of rose quartz through pale pink visualized light in order to facilitate healing, soothing, and self-love. Or, to draw out negativity and activate positive flow throughout your body, you might visualize/imagine/feel that you are sitting on a giant black tourmaline.

While you are free to do this with any of the crystals that you know and love, below you'll find a sampling of crystals that I have found to be especially useful in my energetic magical practice. The only prerequisite to working with these (or any) crystals in your nonphysical practice is to spend some quality time with them in the physical world *first* so that you can call upon the crystal's actual (nonphysical) vibration at will. That way, you can recognize its vibration within you (since we are, in truth, one with everything) and then consciously direct it toward any intention that you choose.

For more information on the metaphysical properties of crystals, I suggest Melody's book series *Love Is in the Earth*.

Amethyst

As a purely positive stone that gently transmutes challenging or disruptive energies into soothing ones, amethyst aligns us with our spirituality and divine connection. You can call upon its vibration for help with sleep, spirituality, emotional healing, stress relief, and healing from addiction.

Aquamarine

Like a clear waterfall in sunlight, aquamarine is soothing, cooling, purifying, and refreshing. It possesses an excellent vibration to call upon for clarity, cleansing, and calm energy.

Aventurine

Vibrant green aventurine resonates at the heart chakra. Its vibration soothes grief, boosts vitality, and helps open our hearts to love. Try continually flooding your heart with soft, cool green aventurine light anytime you feel heartbroken or overwhelmed by grief.

Black Tourmaline

Black tourmaline powerfully activates energy flow while drawing out toxins and negativity. Because it also can be employed as a shield that immediately neutralizes and dismantles negativity, it can be useful for intentions related to protection, especially from long-standing negative energy streams (as in the case of family members with whom you have ongoing issues) or consciously directed negative energy streams (as in the case of negative thoughts or ill wishes continually being sent your way). For this purpose, you might want to visualize yourself or your home within a sphere or circle of black tourmaline first thing in the morning and last thing at night, for as long as necessary.

Citrine

Like an orange grove in sunlight, citrine has a bright, positive, buoyant disposition. Its vibration can be employed to dissipate depression, brighten the mood, and open the door to abundant wealth and prosperity consciousness. Try shining it like sweet, tangerine-tinted sunlight throughout a room or area, or bathing your checkbook in its happy, affluent vibe.

Clear Quartz

Clear quartz is a general purifier and amplifier. Shine clear quartz–enhanced light throughout your body or a space for energetic clearing and to increase positive energy, or direct it through your finger to empower, activate, or amplify the energy contained within an object or charm.

Garnet

Garnet possesses the most sensual and grounding properties of the color red. As a visualized vibration, it can bring us into our bodies and into the present moment, and it can help heal and enhance sexuality, activate passion, and fuel personal empowerment. Try filling your bed with deep red garnet light just after you open your eyes to help you get up and moving. Garnet energy can also be directed into the bloodstream as a complementary therapy to help bolster circulation and circulatory health.

Lapis Lazuli

This vibrant blue vibration can enhance creativity, support communication, and bring healing and happiness to the heart. It's also an excellent energetic tool for soothing, protecting, and uplifting emotionally and spiritually sensitive children. Try surrounding your child with vibrant blue lapis light before school or sending it throughout her room just before bedtime.

Moonstone

This soft white or beige ethereal crystal resonates with the cool, receptive, mystical energy of the moon. Try sending its vibration into your third eye chakra to enhance intuition or moving it throughout your body when you want to experience greater receptivity.

Rose Quartz

Rose quartz is currently my favorite vibration to summon. It helps with self-love, soothes anxiety, heals heartache, relieves physical pain, and generally promotes peace, harmony, and relaxation. While babysitting my nephew, I've also discovered that it is an excellent crystalline vibration to call forth when soothing a crying child or rocking him to sleep.

Herbs and Flowers

Just like with crystals, provided you have a friendly, firsthand relationship with a particular flower or herb, you can call upon that plant's healing and magical properties even when you don't happen to be in its physical vicinity. Again, you can do this with any herb or flower that you choose. To give you some ideas for how to get started, here are some of my favorite plants to call upon for this purpose.

For additional information on herbs and flowers, I suggest checking out my book *The Magic of Flowers* and Scott Cunningham's books *The Encyclopedia of Magical Herbs* and *Magical Aromatherapy*.

Camellia

Visualizing a camellia blossom at your heart center can bolster the heart and boost your energy; so can surrounding yourself in a giant camellia blossom.

Cinnamon

I like to call on the scent of cinnamon (rather than the appearance of it), especially when my intention relates to wealth and prosperity, but the scent of cinnamon—specifically in the form of cinnamon incense—is an extremely powerful tool for improving and purifying vibrations. For this purpose, you might send etheric cinnamon incense smoke around your body or throughout a space.

Jasmine

Simply closing your eyes and envisioning jasmine in bloom, then taking an imagined whiff, can get you out of your head and into your body by activating sensuality and sexual healing. (I feel it immediately in my womb and my knees!) Similarly, the sweet scent and vibration of jasmine can be an excellent enhancement to magical intentions related to romantic love. Envisioning jasmine and calling to mind its scent can also help attract wealth and prosperity.

Lavender

Nothing can tune me into the emotion of joy quite like the inner vision of blossoming lavender in bright sunlight, gently trembling in the breeze, with bees excitedly buzzing from flower to flower. With a vibration that is both soothing and uplifting, it is truly the essence of joyfulness. You might also call to mind the scent of lavender—or infuse your visualized light in it—for relaxation, stress relief, sleep, cleansing, purification, and to release guilt and shame.

Lilac

Blossoming lilac in sunshine, along with the scent of lilac, transports me out of the purely physical dimension and into the place between the worlds of form and spirit. You can call upon the vision or scent of lilac for help with space clearings and exorcisms, to tune into your intuition, and to activate spiritual awareness.

Mint

When I was a child, fresh spearmint grew in our front yard; I just adored plucking their leaves, inhaling their scent, and eating them. Perhaps that's why it's so easy for me to call to mind the scent and vision of fresh mint. I love sending bright green mint leaves through sparkling, pale mint green light to foster a cool, clear, calm state of mind, soothe my spirit, and experience a pleasant burst of invigoration.

Patchouli

I will admit that I don't have a personal relationship with the live patchouli plant. However, I do find calling upon the scent of patchouli (in its essential oil or dried herb form) to be an extremely useful way to get grounded in no time flat.

Rose

With a vibration and symbolism that is pretty much synonymous with love, visualizing the scent and appearance of roses can be a very effective magical technique. Red rose petals are great for romantic love; pink for self-love, sweetness, and friendship; and white for powerful purification.

Rosemary

If you want a shot of energy and clarity or help with sustaining focus over time, simply visualize a fresh rosemary bush in sunlight. Imagine yourself lightly crushing one of its leaves between your fingertips and inhaling the scent, or you can send the vision or visualized scent of rosemary throughout bright white light. This can be helpful for studying, test taking, and any other time a clear and focused mind is of the essence.

Sage

The visualized scent of fresh sage or essential oil of clary sage can bring clarity to the mind and serenity to the emotions. And if you're a fan of smudging with a bundle of dried white sage, you might call upon the inner vision and scent of abundant white sage smoke billowing in and around anything you'd like to spiritually clear. (Bonuses: no fire alarms will go off, no burning embers will fall, no one will think you're smoking pot, and no one will get an asthma attack!)

Sweetgrass

Sometimes I like to smudge with braids of dried sweetgrass or sweetgrass incense in order to open up a doorway of light between this realm and the next. This can be helpful for supporting people or animals as they're transitioning out of this life and into the light or for summoning sweet spirits into a space. If you're familiar with the scent and vibration of sweetgrass smoke, you can summon it energetically for the same purposes.

Sounds

I find that my visualizations often get quite a bit more intense when I add the element of sound. For example, a visualization of fire (or lilac fire) can be nicely enhanced with the sound of crackling flames. Similarly, a visualization of water is great with the sound of ocean waves, a rainstorm, or a bubbling stream. And I love to summon the air element by conjuring up the sound of tinkling bells or wind in the trees. You can also get creative and add, say, the sound of a clear chime to a visualization of mint-scented light blue light or the sound of paper money being counted to a visualization of a swirl of golden sparkles. The possibilities are truly endless...

Other Ingredients

...and I *do* mean endless. There are plenty of etheric ingredients you can add to your rituals and practices that don't neatly fall into any of the categories above. Here are some of them; use these ones if you like or choose your own.

Blood

Blood is highly protective. Moon blood, in particular, is one of the most magically potent substances known to humans; it's highly protective and empowering. So if you'd like, for example, to bless your home with protective energy, you might call up an inner image of your moon blood and then, in your mind's eye, anoint your front door and all other outside doors and windows with the strong intention that absolutely no harm, and only those with positive intentions, may enter. Or, for instant empowerment of a charm or magical tool, you might imagine anointing the tool with moon blood in order to seal your intention to activate it and fill it with magical power.

Champagne

Pink champagne, perhaps with golden sparkles amidst those upwardly moving bubbles, can be employed to fill a space before a party or romantic rendezvous to infuse the event with a light-hearted and celebratory mood.

Coffee

The visualized scent of coffee can be strongly grounding, clarifying, and energizing. You might call on it whenever you need a shot of presence and focus. (Have you ever noticed that just the decision to have coffee is energizing, even before you actually have it?)

Feathers

I like to visualize clean white feathers floating gently around for purposes related to healing, softening, and soothing. You might also consider calling on feathers for aligning with spirit and receiving divine messages.

Honey

Golden, sweet, sticky honey is a great visualization to call upon for prosperity, romance, personal magnetism, or general sweetness. Basically, if it's your intention to be very charming and influential, honey might be a good ally to summon. You can drench yourself in it, see it moving slowly downward throughout your body and aura, or send it through a space.

Incense

Any scent of incense smoke that you like and that feels appropriate for any given magical intention can easily be sent through a space, around yourself or another person, or throughout any color of visualized light. Try frankincense or cedar for space clearing and vibration raising, nag champa for magical consciousness and present-moment awareness, or patchouli for sensuality and wealth.

Salt

Salt is a perennial magical ingredient for purification and protection. You can surround yourself in an etheric circle of salt for protection or cast it mentally into the corners and around the perimeter of a room for space clearing. You can also send it through your aura to clear and neutralize negativity.

Sugar

Sugar is simply the energy of pure sweetness, and it can be employed magically as such. For example, if your place of employment could benefit from a bit more sweetness, you might try sending sparkly white sugar granules through pink light and projecting this light throughout your entire work area. Or, if you own a business, you could construct an etheric doorway made of sparkly white sugary light (placed over the physical doorway) in order to attract customers like sugar attracts ants.

5

Your Unseen Allies

As the saying goes, we are unlimited spiritual beings having a limited human experience. As such, you might say that there is a facet of Who We Really Are that is constantly watching over us, orchestrating details, looking before we leap, and helping manifest our magical intentions into form. Because our limited everyday brains can't perceive the whole mechanism behind this, we ascribe the different names, aspects, and specialties to different aspects of the Divine. This does not diminish the fact that these aspects actually do exist. It merely explains why one person may prefer calling on an angel for the very same reason that another might prefer calling on a Hindu deity. Indeed, the way that our divine helpers and unseen allies appear can shift according to our preferences, personal history, chosen worldview, and even our moods. The finite facets (representations or emanations of the Divine) are ways for us to get to know—and in turn to co-create with—the infinite jewel that is the Divine, with whom we are one.

So, once you take the time to discover the aspects of the Divine (aka your Infinite Self) that speak to you, and once you find ways to connect with them that feel powerful to you, you'll be happy to discover that there are all sorts of beings in the nonphysical realm who are especially suited to help you achieve your magical aims. It takes a lot of the pressure off when you can delegate, especially when you're delegating to someone whom you know to be seriously powerful and absolutely reliable! It's sort of like writing an email requesting assistance and then clicking send, knowing that your help will not fail to arrive in perfect timing. Or, in less metaphorical terms, you can set the intention and then let it go, knowing that it will all be perfectly taken care of. (And the really cool thing about this, of course, is that it's the ideal state of mind to be in after setting any magical intention in motion: you do the magic and then you let it go, allowing divine, unseen influences to perfectly orchestrate the details.)

Now, let me be clear: in most cases you will still need to take action in the physical world. The divine helper on whom you call will be like your copilot; he or she will not take over the wheel completely. But when you have a more relaxed and trusting state of mind—knowing beyond all doubt that you've set the proper magical momentum in motion through calling on your helper—you will be more open to divine guidance, and a natural and harmonious flow will naturally begin to characterize your life experience.

Doors of opportunity will appear. You'll be in the right place at the right time. Your pathway will be open.

If you feel drawn to a being mentioned in this chapter or to another being who has similarly helpful and positive qualities, set aside a little bit of time to get to know him or her. To do so, you might go somewhere quiet where you won't be disturbed, close your eyes, and then simply set the intention to tune into this being's energy. At this time you might also (inwardly or aloud) speak or chant this being's name. Then simply hang out and commune a little. You might offer etheric incense smoke or flowers or just emotionally express gratitude and love. Once you make contact and spend some quality time with one or more allies, you can practice working with them to create positive energetic shifts and manifest the conditions you desire. This chapter is about how to do just that.

Although this is optional, in much the same way that a physical elemental altar can be a great anchor for your non-physical magical endeavors, whenever there is an unseen ally of any kind that you regularly call on, it can be a good idea to have some sort of image of this being in your home. This could be something as simple as a printed-out image taped on your fridge or as elaborate as a statue, mural, or framed painting. As part of your daily meditation, you might take a moment to visit and pay your respects to each representation of your unseen allies. I personally like to light a stick of incense and make my way through my home, blessing each image with a bit of the smoke. You could light a candle and carry it around your home or simply visit each image and say a quick but heartfelt thank you.

Just as with the previous chapters, you can use the following descriptions as general guidelines and jumping-off points as you go about the process of discovering the practices and allies that you like working with best.

Archangels

Perhaps in part because I have lived in the City of Angels, I find the angelic realm to be especially enthusiastic about and suited to helping me with my everyday magical aims. Like my city, they're swiftly operating, immensely sprawling (energetically speaking), and quite in alignment with the searing bright light of the sun. Here are some of the archangels—i.e., heads of the angelic hierarchy—whom I call on the most.

Archangel Michael

I call on archangel Michael every single day to cut any cords of fear or attachment from my body and aura, and to vacuum my body and home of all stuck areas and negativity. He has a sword of light and a glowing vacuum tube of light that he likes to use for these purposes, and they are *very* swift and effective. Very often, I also call on him to surround me, my home, my car, and my loved ones in a very bright sphere of protective royal blue light; this is one of his specialties. Many see Michael as the head archangel (archangels are like the monarchs of the angelic realm), myself included. His energy is almost identical to the pure light and heat of the sun.

On the spirit level, he appears to many as a tall, hand-some, muscular blond man with wings, wielding a glowing sword of light and emanating an aura of fire.

In addition to his sword of light, his vacuum tube of light, and his royal blue shielding light, his specialties include the ability to instantly construct a fiery wall of protection that can effectively shield you, your home, your loved ones, or whatever you choose to protect from any and all negativity. For any of these purposes, simply call on him and request the help that you desire. As you tune into his energy, you might also witness him following through with your request. (This might seem as if you are imagining it, which is fine too, as consciously directing your imagination is a way of energetically creating what is visualized, not to mention that imagination is an excellent portal into actually seeing with the psychic and intuitive senses.)

Archangel Michael is also the patron saint of police offi-cers. I had an amazing experience related to this not long ago. I was walking in the alley behind my apartment build-ing in Venice, carrying my recycling to the recycling bin. On my way, I noticed a man walking my direction who appeared to be particularly frenetic in his movements. He was bang-ing against fences and dumpsters and moving in a zigzag pattern somewhat violently, as if he was on some pretty strong drugs. Although Venice is an iconic hub for all sorts of colorful people and situations (a humorous phrase that's sometimes used to describe it is "where art meets crime"), I rarely felt unsafe in my neighborhood, but this time was an exception. I quickly called on archangel Michael and requested that he walk beside me as a bodyguard. I passed the man without incident, but on the way back to my building, I noticed a police car moving slowly through the alley in my direction (something, incidentally, that I have *never* seen, before or since). Just as I was about to approach my gate, the police car pulled up next to me. Right at that moment, I came upon the man from before, hiding behind a car parked in the alley, apparently preparing to strike. He saw the police car and froze. The officer made a point of watching me as I walked up to my gate and safely closed it behind me. As you can imagine, I wasted no time in thanking Michael profusely for sending that officer!

Archangel Metatron

Metatron's energy is soaring and intense; as an intermediary between divine wisdom and earthly life, he has been described as a towering pillar of fire. (Consider how pillars can be seen as solid, direct connection between heaven and earth, and how fire brings illumination and clears away what no longer serves us.) Just about every time I sit down to write, I call on archangel Metatron before I begin, and I feel his presence immediately. In a balanced and sustained way, he helps keep my focus steady and my divine inspiration flowing. Perhaps this ability has something to do with his role as scribe of the Akashic Records (etheric records that are said to contain all that was, is, and is yet to be). Similarly, you might call on archangel Metatron for help with any intention that requires sustained focus, especially if you tend to get overwhelmed by organization or bogged down by details. All you have to do is incorporate something like this phrase into your magic: "Archangel Metatron, I call on you! Please help me to ____." For example, you might place your hands in prayer pose, say the phrase, and visualize a laserlike pillar of light linking you from earth to heaven, keeping you clearly focused on the task at hand.

Archangel Raphael

When physical healing is of the essence, archangel Raphael is my go-to guy. In my experience, he's synonymous with the radiant, soothing, strengthening, innately wise emerald light of the heart chakra. Indeed, he can be a great ally to call on when performing the emerald heart of healing ritual. Even just a quick "Archangel Raphael, please surround me (or my space or my cat or my friend) with your healing green light" can help restore vitality by providing a considerable boost to the body's natural ability to heal.

Archangel Jophiel

As the angel of beauty and sacred aesthetics, I love to call on archangel Jophiel for help with intentions related to attractiveness, whether personal or environmental. She can also help fuel our ability to notice and appreciate beauty, and can help balance and attune our inner state and energetic patterns so that our life conditions become more picturesque and divinely proportioned. You can envision her calibrating, beautifying energy as a vibrant, sparkly lilac pink.

Other Angels

If pure divine energy is (metaphorically) the light of the sun, archangels might be thought of as the refractions of that sunlight that make up the individual colors of the rainbow. Unlike sunlight, however, divine light is infinite, which means that there is an infinite variety and an infinite number of divine creatures, including angels—divine messengers and emissaries—who can help us with our magical intentions and our daily lives. Here are some ways that you can incorporate them into your magical practice.

Meet Your Guardian Angels

Bringing your relationship with your guardian angel or angels into your conscious awareness can be both spiritually gratifying and magically useful. You can then check in with them on a regular basis to receive guidance about anything you may have missed or simply can't see from your more limited human perspective. They're also excellent friends to have when you're feeling down or could use some comforting.

I suggest meeting him, her, or them during your simple daily alignment practice (from chapter 2). After you've called the spirit element, simply sit with your spine straight and relax with your eyes closed. Then bring into your mind the intention to meet your guardian angels. Once you've done this, focus on an inner image of bright or golden-white light completely filling and surrounding you. When your mind feels clear and centered, ask how many guardian angels you have. You might see or hear the numbers one, two, or three in your mind. Then bring to mind the inten-

tion to learn your angels' names. Keeping your mind open
and focusing on the white light, allow yourself to hear, see,
sense, or know the name(s) of your angel(s). Be open to
the name being something from any culture, perhaps even
something that you've never heard before. (For example,
when I did this exercise, one of my angels had an Italian
name, and another had an Indian name that I had never
heard before that moment.) Repeat once or twice more.
Then spend a little time getting to know each angel. See
how they appear to you in your mind's eye, and ask them
if they have any messages for you. You can do this regularly
during your alignment practice until it feels easy to call up
a connection with your angels easily and swiftly at any time
throughout your day. To keep your relationship strong and
balanced, you might like to offer etheric tokens of thanks to
your angels every now and then, such as flowers or fragrant
smoke. (You might like to get to know their favorites.)

Meet Your Present-Moment Angels

There are also angels who come into your life for various purposes and then leave when their job is complete. It
can be quite illuminating to check in and see if you have any
of these present-moment angels currently in your energy
field, and then to ask their names, get to know them a little
bit, and get an idea of what they're helping you out with.
You can do this anytime you have a few moments to yourself. Simply relax, close your eyes, and make the decision
to align with your truest and most divine self (the part of
you that is one with the Divine). You'll find that when you

make this decision and settle into it, you'll begin to feel perfectly loved and perfectly at ease. Once this occurs, ask your
divine self if there are any present-moment angels currently
hanging around. If one comes to mind (or sometimes they
might appear as a group), get a feeling and inner image of
this angel (or group of angels). See if you can sense a name,
and then ask what this angel is here to help you out with in
your life. Get a feeling for this life lesson, and allow your
conscious connection with this angel to align you with this
lesson in a deep way. When this feels complete, repeat the
process to see if there are other present-moment angels (or
groups) with you at the moment.

For example, when I just did this exercise before I wrote
this section, I learned that I have one angel in my energy
field named Marianina, who is a beautiful, curvy angel with
long, flowing brown hair. She tells me that she's helping me
to feel comfortable with my body and to feel nourished and
loved exactly as I am. Then I got in touch with a handsome,
blond male angel named Bruce (!), who is helping ground,
strengthen, and fine-tune the energy at my heart center
so that I can do my work as a writer and consultant in the
clearest and most helpful possible way.

To revisit the concept that I touched on in the introduc-
tion to this chapter, you don't have to think of these angels
as literal beings, although if you did, you wouldn't be far
off. Nothing is "just" in your mind, because *everything* is in
your mind. That includes this book, your house, the street
you live on, your parents, and your individual identity. Our

minds process this physical reality in the exact same way that they process dreams, so who's to say what's real and literal, and what's not? And who's to say that the contents of a dream or a vision are not as real or as pertinent to your life experience as something that happens in your waking life? The answer is *you*, and only you. The bottom line is that getting in touch with your present-moment angels in this way can be a very valuable healing exercise and can enrich your sense of wonderment, magic, and spiritual support.

Request that Angels Surround Your Home

Just about every day, I call on a circle of angels to surround my home, directing in the positive energies of love, light, clarity, serenity, abundance, romance, creativity, and peace. Then I call on a circle of angels to surround the first circle of angels, facing outward this time so that they can neutralize all negativity and direct any less-than-desirable energies back to their source. You may think that this is an excessive use of angelic force, but I find that it's just about right for my neighborhood (which, as I mentioned, is colorful and exhilarating but can sometimes be spiritually wonky and energetically sketchy), and the angels—being emanations of the Infinite—experience absolutely zero depletion in their energy or their ranks. In fact, they seem to be quite happy to do it, as it's their natural desire to help establish peace and harmony on earth. (You might think of angelic support like sunlight: we can take a walk in the sunshine, run our home on solar power, and let the sunlight dry and bleach our whites all at one time, and the sun doesn't feel depleted or bothered one bit. The sun just keeps on expressing and sharing its essence equally with everyone and everything, the same as it always has since before the dawn of humankind.)

Request that Angels Protect Your Car

As representatives of the swift and all-seeing heavenly realm, angels are especially suited to help with intentions related to travel. As anyone who has a car can undoubtedly relate to, it's one of my daily intentions to protect both my car and everyone in and around my car. That's why, just about every single day, I like to call on six angels to surround and protect my car. Why six? Because it feels right, and also because in feng shui it's the number related to the Helpful People and Travel area, which also relates to the realm of heaven.

Request that Angels Help You Find a Parking Place

This is not usually my parking magic of choice, but I know that a lot of people like to cultivate a relationship with a "parking angel." You can do this by going into a meditative state and asking if there are any angels who would like to help you with your intention to find parking spaces as needed. If one or more arrive in your mind's eye, get to know them, and perhaps offer them (visualized) fragrant smoke or flowers. Then, when you need to find a space, simply call on these parking angels, silently or aloud, and ask them to help you find a perfect spot easily and effortlessly.

Something I really like about this exercise is that it's a reminder that angels don't mind helping with anything at all. They are infinite and entirely committed to helping us experience peace, ease, harmony, and joy, even in the seemingly tiniest of ways. Calling on parking angels and experiencing their divine help in finding a spot (or really doing any kind of parking magic) is a good way to be reminded of our complete and total spiritual support system.

Deities

The number of deities that you can call on to help you with your magical intentions is literally countless. Some people like to find one or two that they like and stick to them or find a matching pantheon from a single culture and work with that group of deities exclusively. I, on the other hand, like to switch it up according to my whim. If the Divine is truly infinite—and that is one point, at least, that all religions seem to agree on—I can't see how it could possibly be offended by being represented in myriad ways and addressed by myriad names. In fact, *not* limiting myself when it comes to deities is an important aspect of my spiritual practice, as it constantly reminds me that the Divine can't be limited—quite the contrary, in fact. While my mind is limited, names are limited, appearances are limited, stories are limited, and religions are limited, the Infinite is most emphatically *not* limited. For me, confining myself to a single name or likeness for the Divine would, in effect, be like saying, "The Infinite is this but not that"—which, of course, is both logically and linguistically incorrect. (This is not to say that I think everyone needs to do it my way; it's just the way that works best for me.)

Since there are countless deities, please don't feel limited to the ones below. I have chosen these because of my special affinity for them and because I have found them to be of great assistance to my magical and spiritual work. If you'd like more inspiration, I highly recommend Judika Illes's lovely and inspiring book *The Encyclopedia of Spirits*.

Aphrodite

The famous radiant-haired Greek goddess of love known as Venus to the Romans, Aphrodite is pure love, attraction, pleasure, and romance. You can call on her for help with setting a romantic mood, connecting with your sensual self, healing your sexuality, or attracting a partner. To petition her for help, in your mind's eye you might visit her as she reclines luxuriously in her beautiful temple and offer her sweet-smelling incense, such as vanilla or sandalwood, or fragrant flowers, such as roses and jasmine.

Bast

The Egyptian cat goddess Bast is a divine champion of independence, a mother goddess, and a fierce protectress of felines. She's also aligned with perfumes, and you might accompany her visualization with the inner conjuring of a strong and sweet fragrance, such as jasmine or neroli. I like to call on her every day to watch over my cats.

Brighid

The great Celtic goddess of fire and hearth, Brighid's bright spirit can be an excellent ally for intentions related to cleansing, passion, protection, empowerment, activation, and magical knowledge. If you're depressed or in a funk, she can come to your aid and fill you with optimism and light. She can also protect your home and bless it with the energies of happiness and warmth. Visualize her as a fiery-haired goddess or call her energy into your magical workings by visualizing a Brighid's cross, a four-armed solar cross constructed of reeds or sticks.

Once you strike up a relationship with Brighid and in your mind's eye honor her with offerings, such as coins, blackberries, or ale, you might visualize her cross as a perpetually flaming solar symbol. You can then place this visualized cross over your third eye or on your front door as a potent mark of protection that repels negativity and ill will.

Forseti

Forseti is a strappingly handsome Norse god who is more than happy to be of assistance when justice is of the essence. In fact, he would rather be called on than not; provided those who petition him are in the right, it is truly his pleasure to help bring about a swift and fair conclusion to matters related to fairness and the law. Simply call on him to intervene and then mentally give him a picture of the situation and why you would like help with it. Though you definitely wouldn't want to be on his bad side, you might think of him as a loving and benevolent father figure who is fiercely protective and also happens to have friends in all the right places. As is fitting for his role as divine and benevolent judge, he is said to dwell in a beautiful hall with a shining silver ceiling and radiant golden pillars.

Ganesh

Ganesh is the elephant-headed deity of the Hindu pantheon. As the "remover of obstacles," he's great to call on anytime you want to get things moving. If you've been buried in busywork, harried by hassles, or bogged down by bureaucracy, Ganesh can help cut through the annoyances and get the energy flowing. He's aligned with the fresh and abundant energy of new beginnings, which is perhaps why he likes to be called on first, before any other deities and at the beginning of any project or voyage. Still, I've found that calling on him anytime I need some activation and swift assistance can be quite helpful. Visualized offerings might include any kind of incense as well as red hibiscus blossoms or brightly colored hibiscus tea.

Krishna

Krishna was the physical incarnation, or avatar, of the principle Hindu god Vishnu, although Krishna's popularity as a deity in his own right has arguably surpassed that of Vishnu in much the same way that the physically incarnate son has widely overshadowed the father God in the Christian religion. He appears as a beautiful blue man with a flute and a peacock feather crown, and is often seen with his earthly love, the beautiful goddess Radha, as a symbol of romantic harmony and bliss.

Krishna is a god of peace, love, harmony, and joy, and he can be especially helpful with banishing negativity, exorcising unsavory deities, bringing wealth and sustenance, bringing harmony to relationships, infusing physical spaces with a feeling of peace, and blessing food (provided it's vegetarian).

Lakshmi

Lakshmi is the gorgeous Hindu deity of wealth and affluence as well as luxury, nourishment, and love. Often pictured near a beautiful stream and with golden coins around her, she reminds us that we are inherently worthy of all the abundant blessings the Universe provides. Call on her to infuse your home, career, consciousness, and life with wealth, prosperity, and blessings of all varieties. You might imagine her arriving with the sound of coins jingling, rushing water, and perhaps a whiff of fresh jasmine. Ganesh and Lakshmi work together often to clear the way for wealth and bring blessings of wealth, respectively.

The Lord and Lady

The Lord and Lady are the archetypal Divine Masculine and Divine Feminine. You might say that they are the dual emanation of the One Infinite Ray; from there, all other deities are emanations of them. They are the yin and yang, the mother and the father, night and day, moon and sun, earth and sky. Every day I like to remind myself—and them—that I am their devotee. By offering myself up to them during my morning meditation and attunement, I remind myself that I am one with All That Is and align my actions and intentions with the Great Spirit.

As they are emanations of the appearance of duality and they are the two universal polarities, they can also be helpful to call on for help with spiritual and emotional balance. They are also quite passionate and are constantly interacting and coupling in order to give birth to all things. For this reason, they can be successfully petitioned for help with romance, creativity, fertility, and abundance. In fact, whatever your intention (provided that it's in alignment with the truest good of all), the Lord and Lady have pretty much got you covered.

As you call on them, you might envision a beautiful horned man and a gorgeous long-haired woman holding each other and dancing, working magic, or kissing. You might also feel the earth beneath your feet as you contemplate the sky over your head or call up an image of the sun and the moon.

Divine couples of various traditions might be seen as their incarnations; for example, the deities Krishna and Radha or the ascended masters Saint Germain and Portia. In Neopagan traditions, their names are many and include the Green Man and the May Queen (or Spring Maiden), Cernunnos and the Triple Goddess, or Dionysus and Demeter/Persephone.

As I mentioned in chapter 3, you can call on the Lord and Lady for help with conjuring the cleansing, balancing, and calibrating lilac fire of transmutation.

Quan Yin

Quan Yin is the Buddhist goddess of peace and harmony. She's also known as the Bodhisattva of Infinite Compassion. (A bodhisattva is someone who chooses to be reborn again and again into this physical plane until all beings find peace.) Her name, which means "the one who responds to the cries of the world," suits her. She has a gentle yet very powerfully healing energy that is evocative of rose quartz and white lotus blossoms. As a counterpart to other healing mother goddesses, such as Mary and Isis, practitioners of many spiritual faiths call upon her for healing of all varieties. She's believed to be a feminine aspect of the beloved Buddhist deity Avalokiteshvara, although some believe her to be the ascended spiritual form of a human princess. Call on her for gentleness, soothing, harmony, heart healing, and healing of all varieties. I've also discovered that she can be a great help with soothing crying children.

Yemaya

Yemaya is the powerful ocean and mother goddess in the Yoruban pantheon. She often appears as a dark-haired mermaid, and she can be petitioned for help with intentions related to love, romance, marriage, wealth, and deep inner cleansing.

For a potent cleansing and releasing ritual, you might envision yourself at the seashore with seven white roses. Call on Yemaya, and see her rise up in the waves to acknowledge your presence. Thank her and ask for help with cleansing your spirit and renewing your soul. Then take one of the seven white roses and walk into the sea, releasing it as an offering of thanks to Yemaya once you're completely immersed in the water, head and all. Walk back out of the water, procure a second rose, and repeat the process until all seven roses are in the ocean, then thank Yemaya from the bottom of your heart.

Ascended Masters

In New Age thought, an ascended master is someone who once walked the earth and has now transitioned into the role of a divine helper who behaves—for all intents and purposes—much like an angel or a deity. In my own personal experience, I have found this to be the same dynamic as that of the saints whom I like to work with. That's why I've classified them as the same thing.

As you begin to explore the realm of the New Age ascended masters, you may notice that there's not always a lot of historical background available on them. This is because ascended masters who appear solely in New Age traditions (and who don't appear first in other traditions) have usually been discovered and explored exclusively on the inner planes. This means that the information that we have on them comes from channeled sources—people who connect with them in the spiritual realm and write down the information they receive.

Here are some of my favorites. I suggest noticing the ones you're drawn to and then relaxing and tuning into their vibration on your own in order to get to know them better. And if you'd like to become acquainted with more ascended masters, I suggest *The Encyclopedia of Mystics, Saints, and Sages* by Judika Illes and *Ascension Magick* by Christopher Penczak.

Lady Nada

A blond woman surrounded by light and holding a pink rose, Lady Nada's wisdom has to do with sound, silence, vibration, communication, femininity, and personal power. Like many New Age ascended masters, I find her vibration to be so high as to be almost inaccessible, but I also like that about her. Like blinding sunlight, she brings a very clear purity to the heart and spirit. She can help with writing, healing oneself or another, regaining power, feeling comfortable with one's femininity, and bringing clarity to any situation through communication and understanding.

Lady Nada's earthly incarnations are said to include a priestess at a temple of love in Atlantis and John the Baptist's mother, Elizabeth.

Portia

Portia is an incarnation of Morgan le Fay or the Lady of Avalon from the Arthurian legends. The role of the Lady of Avalon was an earthly emissary and channel of the Divine Feminine, or the Goddess. Similarly, Portia likes to support us in connecting with the Goddess and in finding our own Divine Feminine flame within. Additionally, as Saint Germain is believed to be an incarnation of Merlin (who is said to have worked magic in concert with the Lady of Avalon), and as the two are both associated in New Age thought with transmutation and the violet flame, they are seen as spiritual and magical partners. (I sometimes like to call on Portia and Saint Germain for the cauldron of lilac fire visualization.)

Her other specialties include justice, wisdom, magical power, and yin-yang balance.

Merlin

The archetypal bearded magician and bard of Avalon and Camelot, Merlin appears in modern mythology as Dumbledore, Gandalf, and Obi-Wan Kenobi. It's as if he's present in the human psyche as the very embodiment of magical and alchemical wisdom. I like to call on him for help with fine-tuning the energy of my home, but he can be called on for any kind of energy work, especially—because he's the ultimate expert—when intricacy and subtlety are of the essence.

Unlike many helpers, Merlin's somewhat picky about who he helps. He prefers to work with serious and committed magical students. But don't be let down if he doesn't arrive; just keep working on your craft day in and day out, and one day you'll call on him and perhaps he'll actually appear. You might think of him as a master teacher: he doesn't show up for the beginning classes—not out of judgment or malice, but simply because it's not time for him to share his wisdom with you yet.

When you call on him—provided he chooses to appear—you may notice in your mind's eye that he likes to work with rainbow light and sacred geometry. The rainbow light possesses a calibrating wisdom that knows exactly what fine-tuning is needed, and the sacred geometrical patterns he chooses are always significant to the situation. If you can notice what they are in your mind's eye and then research their significance through meditation and actual study, it can be quite illuminating. And thus the master teacher passes along not only magic, but also magical understanding.

Saint Francis of Assisi

Saint Francis is an eleventh- and twelfth-century spiritual pioneer famous for his connection with animals. It's my sense that if he were alive today, he would be a Pagan. He was able to practice his seemingly earth-based spirituality without finding himself tortured, imprisoned, or killed— although others in his order of Franciscan monks tragically did suffer such a fate—and even preserved his teachings through his legend, writings, and poetry. The story goes that right before he died, he thanked his donkey, who then wept actual tears. An early proponent of vegetarianism and animal rights, he is often pictured among animals and is well known for preaching sermons to the birds. I call on Saint Francis just about every day to watch over my cats and to keep them safe, and he can also be invoked to protect and bless any other species of animal friend. Other kinds of animal-related challenges also fall under his patronage, such as unwanted rats or other animals on your property, as he specializes in finding solutions that don't involve any sort of harm. To cultivate a relationship with him on the inner plane, in lieu of offerings (which he isn't particularly interested in anyway), you might meet with him and profess your commitment to animal welfare and a cruelty-free lifestyle.

Saint Germain

Saint Germain is a beloved New Age master (he's not a Catholic saint—"Saint" just happens to be part of his name) who always appears with intensely cleansing violet flame, which transmutes negativity into positivity and love. He's so beloved, in fact, that he may even be seen as the spiritual harbinger, instigator, and reigning monarch of the New Age. His story is quite remarkable and contains actual historical elements.

He's said to be the ascended spiritual form of a real-life count and courtier who lived in Europe in the mid 1700s. By alternating accounts, he was an alchemist, a "Wonderman" (according to Voltaire, who meant it sarcastically), a compulsive liar, and a con artist. Others believed that he could change base metals into gold and that he was five hundred or more years old. What's generally agreed upon is that he was quite popular as well as knowledgeable: he was a frequent guest among the royal courts, he knew all the European languages, and he was an accomplished musician.

Interestingly, starting with Helen Blavatsky and the Theosophical Society and continuing until the present day, he has become quite the superstar in the spiritual realms as a being of great wisdom, compassion, and spiritual power. He is said to be the reincarnation of many prominent men, including Merlin, Saint Francis of Assisi, and Francis Bacon. (I can definitely see him being a reincarnation of Merlin, although he has his own unique personality and energetic signature.)

As an alternative or enhancement to the cauldron of lilac fire exercise, you can call on him to fill your home, your body, or any situation with vibrant, transmuting violet flame. And, as I've mentioned, you can also call on Saint Germain and Portia (who is seen as his "twin flame," a feminine counterpart to his masculine energy) as the god and goddess for the cauldron of violet fire exercise.

Ancestors and Deceased Loved Ones

Sometimes our ancestors and deceased loved ones like to step forward from the spirit world in order to help us out in our daily lives. This isn't a decision *we* make, although we can strengthen the bond if we so choose. Rather, it's a decision made by the ancestor or loved one. The way we know that they're present is that we see them in a vision or get a strong feeling or sign that they are hanging around. (This is not to be confused with an earthbound entity, or ghost, that has not passed into the light and is hanging around due to fear or confusion. You can tell the difference because the former gives you a boost of positive energy, while the latter may deplete you or cause you to feel unhappy or drained.)

Although no one's physical personality is without flaw, my experience with ancestors who are in this plane of existence is purely positive. In my case, it appears to me as if it is part of their karmic process to help me out, often in ways that may help remedy some of the decisions they made in their parenting of my parents. (The helpful ancestors with whom I have the strongest relationship both happen to be grandparents.)

This doesn't appear to be out of guilt or punishment, however, but out of joy. In fact, they seem much more joyful and at peace to me than I ever saw or heard about them being on this side of the veil.

One of the loveliest things about having a relationship with deceased loved ones is that it reminds me of that place beyond our world where we are washed in light and reminded that all is love, and that we are not, in fact, separate from anyone or anything. Connecting with their beneficent forgiveness of themselves and All That Is reminds me to forgive and release my attachments to the finite, drama-related stuff that really doesn't matter anyway.

To work with your ancestors or deceased loved ones in a magical way, strengthen your relationship by connecting with them during meditation. I often feel their messages as loving emotions or receive their messages via pictures and symbols that they show me rather than have actual verbal conversations with them, although your experience may be different. Giving them offerings (in your mind's eye) of things that they liked during life can be a nice way to offer gratitude and strengthen the bond. Then as the situations arise, you can call on them for help with the things that they most like to help you with; for example, my Grandma Cecey likes to help me with my physical health as well as shopping and finding pretty clothes, while my Papa Harry seems to be all about helping me heal my relationship with my womanhood and feminine power.

Faeries

While angels are emanations of the divine realm of heaven and the sky, faeries are emanations of the divine realm of nature and the earth. In other words, angels are aspects of pure potentiality and the divine unmanifest, while faeries are aspects of the finite, manifest world. This means that they are more like humans (with egos and such), and less like swift and reliable nonphysical helpers such as angels and divinities.

Still, they possess a magic all their own, and if you choose to incorporate them into your magical practice, you'll find that they have a lot of blessings to share. I've found that rather than asking faeries for help, it's better to cultivate strong relationships with them and then allow them to bestow their favors and blessings according to their whims. Here are some ways to do just that.

Ally with the Faeries in Your Neighborhood

Because faeries are the spirits of nature and the earth, they are closely tied to physical places. Making a point of allying with the faeries who live in your neighborhood can help you feel grounded, protected, and inspired. Just like having strong positive relationships with your human neighbors, making friends with your faerie neighbors will help you feel loved, supported, and at home in the world. It will also help fuel your positivity, energy, prosperity, and luck.

To ally with the faeries in your neighborhood, take walks and spend time outdoors regularly—perhaps at least four to five times per week, as weather permits. Even if you're in a city, notice flowers, trees, and critters, and give them your loving attention. Stop and smell the flowers, listen to the birds, and chat with neighborhood cats. For extra brownie points (pun intended), you can leave shiny silver coins, pretty crystals, or walnut shells full of ale or champagne near flowers or trees. As your relationship with the faerie realm grows, you may notice that your intuition is heightened with regards to regularly making decisions that open doors to increased happiness, romance, and wealth.

Commune with Faeries in Natural Settings

Another excellent way to strengthen your relationship with the faerie realm is to spend "alone" time in a serene natural setting and quietly tune into the details: the light as it dances on water, the sound of wind in trees, the gently treading deer, the scampering squirrels, and the clouds moving gently across the sky. Faeries especially love it when you commit to helping the environment, so you might declare your commitment to do so, silently or aloud. If you notice any trash in the area where you are, picking it up would be an excellent way to honor the faeries' presence. As a physical investment in your nonphysical relationship, you might also leave them gifts, as described above.

The "Little Man"

I wish I knew the name of the woman who taught me this "little man" ritual for finding temporarily missing objects, but alas, I do not. Years ago, I was taking an herbal healing class at a women's gathering in the woods, and a very wise woman shared it with the group. I have made it my own (as you must), but I am so grateful to her for passing along the wisdom. Now, I pass it along to you.

In this visualization, you will be calling upon the part of your mind that knows all and sees all (who is indeed a very helpful ally), and you will be assigning an inner vision and personality to this part of your mind. For me it is actually a little man, although I have heard of people for whom it is a computer, a tree, a filing clerk, or a fairy princess. Please do not feel limited by the name.

To illustrate how this works, I'll explain my personal "little man" exercise to you. When I am trying to find a temporarily missing object, such as my keys, I stop my frantic rushing around, close my eyes, and take some deep breaths. Then I visualize myself in an elevator, going up, up, up, and up. I watch an old-fashioned little arrow showing me that I'm going to the very top floor, and then I hear a "ding" indicating that I've arrived. When the doors slide open, I see that I'm in a Plexiglas room at the top of an extremely tall skyscraper in New York City. I push open the swinging door and feel the air whip around me as I walk to the edge of the roof. There, hovering over the city between two skyscrapers, is a meditating little man who is dressed like a genie. I say to him, "Little man, where are my keys?"

He doesn't say anything, but I know that he's heard and that he will bring what I need to know into my consciousness. Then I thank him (sometimes mentally burning him incense or offering him flowers, both of which hover in front of him in honor of his help) and turn back toward the elevator. I open my eyes and continue to go about my day without stressing out too much about the object, although I may still look for it, just with confident nonchalance rather than panic. Almost invariably I find it within minutes.

To find your little man (or whatever he/she/it is for you), simply close your eyes and relax, setting the intention to see a visual representation of the part of your mind that knows, sees, and remembers everything. Notice the process of approaching this being, and then ask your question. Notice how your version of the little man responds (or doesn't). Know in your heart that your little man has heard and is now diligently processing your request. Thank your little man, perhaps giving him an offering of thanks, and then go on your way. After opening your eyes, see if you can do something other than actively look for the object, or at least do so without panic.

Conjured Creatures

Sometimes it can be helpful to conjure a creature (or several) out of thin air to help you with an intention. In other words, out of the divine unmanifest or conscious amniotic light (out of which all beings, seen and unseen, arise), you can employ the power of your mind and alliance with the Divine to envision and then breathe life into your own personal menagerie of magical helpers.

Here are some examples for how you might do this.

Protective Lions

You know those protective lion statues that some people like to put on either side of their front door? Perhaps you'd like to protect your home with energetic lions instead. To do this, during a waxing moon, relax your body and close your eyes. Envision two glorious lions. They can be male (with a mane), female (without a mane), or one of each. They can be normal lion color or any color of the rainbow, according to what feels most powerful for you. Envision each of them until they are very strong in your mind; visualize cosmic light from above and earth light from the core of the earth flowing down and up respectively and meeting to breathe life into your visualization. Christen them with names, and then interact with them as if they are newly adopted family members. Pet them, send them love, and offer them food, water, and gifts. Then ask if they would mind watching over your home (since you created them for this purpose, they will say yes) and making sure only people with the most positive intentions can enter. Then station them on either side of your front door. Replenish their energy regularly by thanking them by name and spending time with them on the internal plane.

Guardian Wolf

In a similar way, you might conjure a wolf to walk with you (or perhaps one of your children) always, in order to powerfully protect you from any possible harm.

Lucky Unicorn

In the same way that I suggested conjuring the lions in the previous exercise, you might conjure a colorful unicorn to stay with you always, leading you toward luck, magic, and positive experiences.

Circle of Horses

Perhaps you need very powerful protection for your aura, a strong dose of positivity and vitality, and an overall energetic boost. For these purposes, you might conjure eight horses of various colors: red, orange, yellow, green, blue, indigo, pink, and violet. If you are an artist, you might draw eight horses (without color yet) or you can also print them out as coloring pages from the Internet. Wait until you find images that feel right to you, choosing unicorns, pegasi, regular horses of any variety, or any combination thereof. Then arrange them around you in a circle on the floor so that the horse that will be red is pointing north; orange, northeast; yellow, east; green, southeast; blue, south; pink, southwest; indigo, west; and violet, northwest.

Then, while playing music, take your time and color each horse according to your inner vision, starting with red and moving in a clockwise direction. Name each horse. Then visualize earth light coming up from the core of the earth and cosmic light coming down from above and merging and breathing life into your vision. Take some time with your eyes closed to spend some time with each horse, getting to know him or her a little bit. Then, when you're out in the world or as you're drifting off to sleep, anytime you feel that you could use powerful protection and a boost of positivity, call each to mind and then call them by name. See the red horse before you, the yellow to the right of you, the blue behind you, and the indigo to your left (and each other horse in between, respectively). You can also ask them to stay with you always, and then, throughout the day, close your eyes or simply tune in to see if any of them have any messages for you.

You can also adapt this exercise to feature a different type of animal that feels powerful for you.

6

Aligning with the Infinite

While this life experience is characterized by the appear-ance of duality, in truth all is one. We are each a unique and inextricable component of the Infinite, just as the Infinite resides within our every cell. When we know this deeply and live with this holistic awareness, our life comes into greater and greater harmony and balance. We are more often awake and alert to the subtle and unspoken messages that are interwoven into the world around us. And while we still encounter challenges, we feel that we can move through them courageously, and we emerge stronger and wiser than we otherwise would have been.

Outer Symbols and Visitations

Just as you are not separate from the Infinite, you are not separate from the world around you. Neither is the world around you separate from you; indeed, each reflects and contains the other. Because of this, and because like attracts like, one of the most basic ways of discerning divine messages is through a recurring, seemingly coincidental encounter with a particular thing, such as a symbol, image, word, number, plant, story, or creature. Because the forms that this may take are truly endless, and because the symbolism of any given item will be at least slightly different for everyone, I think the best way for me to begin to give you an idea of how this works is to give you a few examples from my own life; at the end of the section, I'll walk you through receiving these types of messages on your own. Please notice that the Universe does not communicate with us in the same way that our buddies do; while the messages can sometimes be quite clear, they are often more of a validation or gentle nudge, calling attention to a pattern or putting your mind at ease rather than unequivocally conveying a point.

The Lingam Keychain

Not long after I wrote a popular blog post about Chinese New Year and the Year of the Yang Wood Horse (a masculine year that is aligned with forward movement and the wood element), I had lunch with my girlfriend Angela, who had just returned from a yoga retreat in Bali. She gifted me with a lovely, extremely auspicious-feeling wooden souvenir keychain shaped like a penis, painted teal (a color associated with the wood element) and embellished with a flower (also associated with the wood element). She told me that, because of the fact that the god Shiva is honored in Bali, wooden lingams (as they are called) are quite popular spiritual items in the region. I loved it, especially because I had recently been paying special attention to honoring the Divine Masculine principle as well as my own sacred sexuality. The next day, as I ran on the beach holding my keys (along with the keychain), I encountered a small penis keychain that just happened to be washed up on the shore at exactly the point at which I first approached the edge of the waves. I interpreted this as double validation of my excitement about the Lunar New Year as well as my inner nudge to study and honor the Divine Masculine principle. Because lingams are considered lucky and represent fertility, pure potentiality, and new beginnings, I also interpreted it as a highly auspicious omen for the new lunar year ahead!

Although there were only two lingam keychain visitations, lingam keychains were not something I was at all accustomed to seeing or hearing about, so two of them making their way into my awareness within twenty-four hours was obviously out of the ordinary and worth paying attention to.

The Number 444

More often than I notice any other number, I seem to notice the number 444. I notice it on license plates, clocks, and numerous other places. According to Doreen Virtue, this number is a reminder that angels are with you. Indeed, when I see the number it often seems to be when I am rushing around or worried about something, and it instantly puts my mind at ease. I feel it reminding me that all is well: everything is divinely orchestrated, everything is occurring in perfect timing, and I'm exactly where I'm meant to be.

And when I see it numerous times in succession, I am especially aware that the Divine is telling me to relax because everything is unfolding just exactly as it should.

Butterflies

I often see butterflies flittering across my path or above my car. This always feels like a sign that the faeries are near and that they're bestowing their lucky and magical blessings upon me. It also reminds me to slow down and enjoy the day. If I happened to be worrying or hurrying, a butterfly always reminds me to come into the present moment and to let my mind be at peace.

Similarly, when something comes into your awareness that shifts you out of one mindset and into another, see if you can get the message from the Universe that goes along with that symbol. That way, you're opening up the line of communication and establishing your own personal language with the Infinite.

White Buffalo Calf Woman

Years ago my boyfriend Ted and I got in a horrendous fight. Suffice it to say that in retrospect I realized it was much ado about nothing, while at the time it felt really serious and painful. When I did a card reading on it, I drew a card from my Archangels and Ascended Masters deck called White Buffalo Calf Woman that counseled me to make peace and forgive. I promptly ignored it and drove to my dad's for the weekend. As soon as I entered the guest room where I always sleep, I saw something that had not been there before: a large framed picture of White Buffalo Calf Woman holding out a peace pipe—and it was *the exact same artwork* that was in my deck. Clearly, White Buffalo Calf Woman was refusing to let her message of peace and reconciliation be ignored.

Now, some of you may be thinking that this was just a coincidence because clearly the reason the picture was there was because my father put it there, and this brings up an important point. Please notice that this type of thinking (the cause is this and therefore it can't be that) is the result of a linear and limited construct of thought. In reality, everything is connected. My dad is part of the Universe. So was the yard sale where he found the picture. So was my decision to go visit him at that particular time. So all of those so-called "causes" of my encounter with White Buffalo Calf Woman were inextricably interwoven with All That Is. To put this another way, in magical thought, just as in more modern scientific thought (such as in the field of quantum physics), just because cause A contributed to effect B, this does not exclude other possible causes.

Identifying External Symbols and Visitations

My acquisitions editor at Llewellyn, Elysia Gallo, has pointed out that readers may be thinking something like "I keep seeing pigeons everywhere; what does it mean?"—when, in fact, it might simply mean that pigeons are very common in your area! And this is an excellent point. It's important to remember that an external symbol or visitation is notable only when it feels uncommon in some way. A wild parrot in a neighborhood where wild parrots are rare is most definitely something to pay attention to. And just because they may be common, we still wouldn't want to write off the pigeons altogether! If a pigeon lands on your head, a flock of pigeons seems to inexplicably follow you as you walk down the street, or a pigeon poops on your shoulder three days in a row, it's obvious that you've got a message in there somewhere. And even if a pigeon or group of pigeons flies into your awareness in a seemingly non-spectacular way but you feel an unmistakable inner nudge to pay attention, you've got a message there too. But regularly encountering a bunch of pigeons in an area where pigeons always like to hang out, without any inner nudge or anything else out of the ordinary, is not likely a divine message.

Another important key to discerning a valid symbol or visitation is to be alert and awake to your inner thought process. For example, if you notice that you're feeling unsure about whether or not you should go ahead and invest in that trip to Hawaii, and right then you happen to glance ahead of you in traffic and you notice a Hawaii license plate or a license plate frame that says *Aloha Spirit*, go ahead and receive that message from the Universe: Hawaii, here you come.

And if you're really looking for guidance in a certain life area, and you'd like to receive it in the form of a symbol or visitation in the physical world, here's an idea: just ask! After relaxing and centering your mind, asking might go something like this:

*Great God/Goddess/All That Is, please help me with
[this situation] by sending me a sign in the physical
world. Please make this sign obvious, unmistakable,
and timely, and help me to open up my consciousness
to receive it in the best possible way. Thank you.*

Once you say this little prayer, it's important to release
your fear and worry around the issue and know that by
enlisting the help of the Divine and by making your request
specific yet open-ended, you have activated the help that
is precisely ideal for you in every way. Trust that you will
receive the message easily and in perfect timing. You can
even forget about your prayer altogether, with assurance
that once the sign appears, you will be reminded of exactly
what you need to know.

Please note that remembering your request and then
searching desperately for a sign is a good example of what
you *don't* want to do, as that leaves your linear, limited mind
in charge, which is exactly what you wanted to transcend by
requesting divine help in the first place. Let go and let the
divine assistance flow!

INTERPRETING EXTERNAL
SYMBOLS AND VISITATIONS

Interpreting symbols and visitations is easy, especially if
you don't overthink it. You're connected with everything,
remember, so the message from the Universe may seem to
be appearing outside of you, but it's also present within you
in its entirety. So if you noticed a symbol or visitation but

don't yet know what it means, just ask yourself to tell yourself a story about what it might mean. Our wisest spiritual selves speak in the language of symbols and stories, so bypass the mind that wants to be "right" and allow your wisest self to tell you a story about, for example, that pigeon who pooped on your shoulder three days in a row. You might say to yourself, "If I were that pigeon, what would I be trying to say?" Then just make up a story. You can even grab your notebook and a pen and make up three different stories about what that pigeon might be trying to tell you. There will be some sort of clue or kernel of truth in all of them. You might say this is because the subconscious transcendent mind is not limited by singular answers or linear lines, but rather thinks in circles and in many dimensions and directions at once.

Of course, some messages and visitations, like the visitation I received from White Buffalo Calf Woman, will be obvious; others may take a little sleuthing. But with practice, interpreting clues from the external world will become easier and easier, and then one day you'll realize that you don't even have to think about it because it's become like second nature—because you've created a passageway between your conscious and subconscious minds and become fluent in the language of symbols.

Inner Symbols and Visitations

When you start to become familiar with the practice of looking within, visualizing, and working magic energetically (and if you faithfully practice the exercises in this book, believe me: you *will*), you will naturally become alert to inner symbols and visitations that will be just as significant for divinatory purposes—or more so—than the symbols and visitations that manifest on the physical plane. Again, the forms that this can take are endless, so to illustrate, here are some more examples from my own life.

Hanged Man

I once spoke with a friend who was going through a transition with her relationship to her career. As I spoke to her, I kept seeing an image of the Hanged Man from the tarot, which clearly communicated to me that it would be helpful for her to surrender to the transition and to the process of letting the old fall away to make room for the new. While it was a challenge, if she could surrender to the process of intense change, I could see—thanks to the Hanged Man— that it all would unfold more easily.

Krishna and Radha

During a feng shui consultation for a client who wanted to manifest a romantic relationship, when I considered what to recommend for various areas, an image of Krishna and Radha, divine lovers from the Hindu pantheon, kept popping into my mind. I ended up recommending décor featuring the two deities more than once, and I felt that it was simply a visitation from the pair, communicating that they wanted to help her experience a beautiful romance.

Mermaid

Ted and I recently went to a vacation cabin in a little town called Ojai for two nights. The morning before we left, as I meditated, I kept seeing a mermaid swim into my mind. I got the strong impression that she was bestowing gifts of prosperity and cleansing. When we arrived at the cabin, there was a stream running right behind it, and then clouds rolled in and it proceeded to rain hard for almost the entire time we were there. The stream turned into a raging torrent, and flood warnings ensued. Despite the unconventional vacation weather, I found it to be a profoundly beautiful couple of days and definitely felt cleansed and blessed by the water and the whole experience. The memory of the mermaid's visitation was both a harbinger and a strong validation of this feeling.

Volcano

As I mentioned earlier in the book, my Papa Harry (my mother's father) is one of my unseen ancestral helpers. During my meditations, he often appears with a Hawaiian shirt on, standing happily and without fear in front of a volcano that is about to erupt. During his lifetime he had four daughters, and it is perhaps an understatement to say that he was not the most supportive guy when it came to allowing them to express their anger, their sexuality, or their feminine power.

The message of the volcano visitation comes through loud and clear: "It is safe to express your anger! It is safe to be powerful and to let your passion and your sexuality flow." It is quite a poignant vision, as I can feel his joy at being able to remedy and restructure one of the challenging karmic patterns he helped set in motion in my ancestral past.

IDENTIFYING INTERNAL
SYMBOLS AND VISITATIONS

At this point, you've probably begun to get the picture that the magical mindset outlined in this book entails vigilant attention to your thoughts, feelings, and inner nudges. While at first this might seem distracting or like a chore, in time it will come to feel natural and you will wonder how you ever got along without it. Your daily attunement practice will certainly help with aligning your conscious and subconscious awareness, as will regularly peering into the depths of your mind to notice if any images or messages come floating to the surface, like the triangle in a Magic 8 Ball. This can be especially helpful when you're considering a particular challenge or issue.

Let's try it now. Relax your body and consider an area of your life in which you would like guidance. Now, without thinking or worrying too much about it, notice if any images, thoughts, feelings, or words come floating into your mind. Please don't dismiss anything you notice: it's very likely that the symbol or visitation you receive will not make sense to you at first. The trick here really is about trusting yourself and trusting the imagery, feeling, or thoughtform that makes itself known to you.

When a message is very strong, the symbol or visitation will present itself again and again, in different ways or in the same way, as you continue to look within with regards to the issue or challenge.

INTERPRETING INTERNAL SYMBOLS AND VISITATIONS

Once you've noticed one or more symbols, images, or thoughts float into your awareness, see if you can discern what they may be trying to tell you. If it's not immediately obvious, you might ask yourself things like:

- What does this symbol, image, or being mean to me?

- What story comes to mind when I think of this?

- How might this apply to this circumstance?

- How do I feel when I consider this?

If what you receive still doesn't seem to make sense, just make a note of it and see if it makes sense to you later; it very likely will. With repeated practice, and as you consistently trust yourself and the symbols and visitations you receive, your rapport with the universal messages and your deep inner wisdom will become more and more pronounced.

Dream Interpretation

The God/Goddess/All That Is—also known as the Universe or the part of us that is one with everything—communicates with our limited everyday mind through dreams. In many ways, dreams provide a direct line to our limitless selves. While there are plenty of books about dream symbols and how to interpret dreams, I have found that the most effective method is the one that my boyfriend Ted taught me. When I tell him my dream, he simply asks, "Well, what do you think that means? I mean, if you had to guess?" It's pretty miraculous, actually: even when I think I have absolutely no idea about what it means, as soon as I start answering him, I discover that I'm actually an *expert* on what it means. Try it!

Symbols are different for everyone, and your subconscious is obviously very specific to you. So, while someone who knows you really well might be able to shed light on the meaning of your dream, chances are good that if you bypass your linear, logical mind with the phrase "I mean, if you had to guess?" you will be the ultimate expert on interpreting your own dreams. Then you can receive all sorts of nifty guidance about how you really feel, how you emotionally interpret various characters and situations in your life, what issues your subconscious mind is currently working out, and even useful hints and tips about how to solve problems and deal with things effectively in the present and future.

Here are some additional things to keep in mind when interpreting your dreams:

- As Starhawk says, "Where there's fear, there's power." Indeed, when a dream really frightens you, it's certainly touched on something that your waking mind doesn't want to look at. Your mind often brings these things up during your dream state so that you can deal with them and retrieve the power that has been hidden beneath your fear. For example, I've had what seems like a million dreams about the end of the world, which used to scare me silly. Now when I dream about the end of the world it's always a happy occasion where life seems to be boiled down to its truest essence, which is love. This lack of fear about whatever the fate of the world may be during my lifetime has definitely carried over into my waking life as well, during which I constantly remind myself to keep my mind on the important things: gratitude and love.

- Frightening characters in dreams can sometimes be aspects of yourself that you don't want to look at or accept in waking life. If this resonates for you, see if you can begin to recognize and then integrate these aspects.

- When you wake up from a dream with tears on your face, it means that a healing has taken place or that you've connected with an actual being (such as a deceased family member or other loved one) on the other side during your dream state.

- When you wake up laughing, it means that you've experienced a crown chakra healing during your sleep: you've connected with the realm of the divine and eternal, and seen beyond the illusory veil of time.

- Lucid dreaming, especially when it seems to take place in the actual physical area in which you're sleeping, and particularly when you are flying in the dream, may actually be astral traveling. This means that an aspect of your consciousness is lifting away from your body and having adventures in a parallel plane. If this happens to you frequently, experiment and see what kinds of interesting things you can learn about the world around you. Check out the physical landscape during your dream and then see how it matches up in waking life. This kind of experimentation can be a wonderful way to enhance your spiritual consciousness, psychic abilities, and magical power.

- Recurring dreams and recurring themes are always especially significant. Pay special attention to them.

Look Ma, No Cards

A lot of us magical folk love using tarot or oracle cards, and I'm no exception. But when your deck of cards is at home or it's just not appropriate to use it at any given moment, no problem! If you have a deck that you know well and use often, simply clear your mind, consider your question or quandary, and watch your mind's eye for a card image from the deck to rise into your consciousness.

Play with this a bit: you might find that shuffling the deck in your mind's eye and then drawing one helps, or (if you're like me) you'll just like to wait for an image to float to the top of your mind. This technique lends itself well to a single-card reading, although you might also try a simple three-card reading where the first card indicates the past or the underlying cause of the issue, the second indicates the present or the main aspect of the issue, and the third indicates the future or the recommended course of action regarding the issue.

If you don't have a deck that you know and love, or if you just want to open your mind to even more possibilities, you can do the same technique but allow any image, symbol, or word to float to the top of your mind. Chances are, once you receive an image (and please trust it, whatever it is, even if you think you made it up), you'll understand its significance. If you don't, just apply Ted's famous dream interpretation technique, and ask yourself, "If I had to guess, what would it mean? How would it apply?"

Take a Walk

While taking a walk might not seem as glamorous as, say, dream interpretation or reading tarot cards without a deck, I have found that it can be just as effective, if not more so, when it comes to aligning with the Universe and gleaning the divine wisdom at the heart of it all.

For a huge percentage of the time that humans have been present here on earth, after all, we have spent most of our time outdoors, and even when we were inside, we were in structures that were much more organically connected with the earth, such as caves and huts made of natural materials.

Ever wonder why food tastes so much better outside? It's because our digestive process literally works better when we're more relaxed and oxygenated, and also because our attunement to all the various movement and scents that surround us opens up our senses more fully to the food's savory subtlety and depth. In much the same way, the oxygen, sights, sounds, and smells of the outdoors remind us of our interconnection and allow us to experience a deeper understanding of ourselves and the world around us. Not to mention, simply stepping outside of your little residential environment literally provides a fresh perspective. You might say it's a way of instantly thinking outside the box.

What's more, the soles of our feet are extremely receptive to the energy of Mother Earth and imbibe spiritual wisdom and nourishment that brings great benefits on all levels. More than a hundred years ago, the famous Sioux chief Luther Standing Bear said,

The old people come literally to love the soil, and they sat or reclined on the ground with a feeling of being close to a mothering power. It was good for the skin to touch the earth and [they] liked to remove their moccasins and walk barefoot on the sacred earth.

This sentiment was reinforced in an article by Gaéton Chevalier, et. al., entitled "Earthing: Health Implications of Reconnecting the Human Body to the Earth's Surface Electrons," where we learn that

[i]t is an established, though not widely appreciated fact, that the Earth's surface possesses a limitless and continuously renewed supply of free or mobile electrons. The surface of the planet is electrically conductive (except in limited ultradry areas such as deserts), and its negative potential is maintained (i.e., its electron supply replenished) by the global atmospheric electrical circuit...

Throughout history, humans mostly walked barefoot or with footwear made of animal skins. They slept on the ground or on skins. Through direct contact or through perspiration-moistened animal skins used as footwear or sleeping mats, the ground's abundant free electrons were able to enter the body, which is electrically conductive. Through this mechanism, every part of the body could equilibrate with the electrical potential of the Earth, thereby stabilizing the electrical environment of all organs, tissues, and cells.

Modern lifestyle has increasingly separated humans from the primordial flow of Earth's electrons. For example, since the 1960s, we have increasingly worn insulating rubber or plastic soled shoes, instead of the traditional leather fashioned from hides.

Indeed, a number of studies have shown that walking barefoot outside blesses us with numerous perks, including significantly reducing the stress hormone cortisol, which in turn strengthens one's immune system and overall state of mind. So if there's a place where you can safely walk on grass or sand, even for just a short distance, do it!

In my area there are a lot of excellent hiking spots, but I more often enjoy simply walking around my neighborhood. It allows me to expand my world: I'm reminded that I don't just live in four walls and a roof, but I'm a part of a neighborhood populated by a whole ecosystem of trees, flowers, grass, squirrels, birds, cats, dogs, and other people.

If I've been struggling with a certain conundrum or issue and I bring it to mind as I walk, it's approximately twenty times more likely that a solution or approach that I feel great about will come whooshing into my awareness. As an added bonus, my route includes a lovely little grassy park. I like to slip off my shoes as soon as I get there—and to leave them off until I get to the other side—to allow my bare feet to soak up the energy, wisdom, and healing power of the earth.

1: HOLISTIC ENERGY MAGIC FOUNDATIONS

The Everyday Sacred

We are perfectly free to think of our everyday life as mundane and label only those moments in which we are doing something out of the ordinary as magical, but that would be based on an illusion. I call it "the illusion of mundane." It's quite a pervasive illusion in our current cultural climate, and it's one that we're all bound to be seduced by now and again (like when we're washing the dishes or in line at the DMV), but it's still an illusion. In truth, there is no such thing as mundane: this life experience is completely and utterly wondrous. What's more, it's mysterious, magical, magnificent, astonishing, and transcendent. Yes, we will forget that sometimes, but that doesn't mean that it's not always true.

This is the heart of my spiritual path and of the teachings contained within this book: to recognize the magic in everything and to express and channel the power contained within this recognition as much as possible, all the time. This means that not just our obvious magical workings, but also *everything* we do—no matter how habitual or commonplace—is an opportunity to celebrate the Great Holy Mystery, to express our power to create positive change, and to honor the enchantment in each moment and in everything.

Clean the House to Clear the Way

Every time you clean the house—or even every time you clean any part of the house—you can do so with an intention. For example, let's say you want to make some new friends. Before you clean the kitchen, you can think, "I'm cleaning the kitchen with the intention to create space for new friends to come into my life." Then you can put on some fun music, light a stick of cinnamon incense (or something warm and cozy feeling), and clean. As you wipe the counter you can think, "I'm clearing the way for new friends," and as you clean the stove you can think, "The shinier this stove gets, the more irresistibly I will draw wonderful new friends into my life experience."

Or you can be less specific and simply clean with the deep inner knowing that the cleaner your house is, the more easily and swiftly blessings of all varieties will come flowing into your life in abundance.

The Inner Speed Limit

A challenging symptom of our current cultural climate is that we can feel drawn into the mindset of multitasking and rushing around so much that we lose sight of the joy and inspiration that is our natural state. Sometimes when I notice myself slipping into this, I can take a step back and also notice that it's not even helping me move faster anyway! I try to wash the dishes faster, and then I break a dish and have to clean it up—or I'm so distracted by what I'm supposed to do in an hour that I forget important parts of the task I'm doing in the present and have to go back and do the task all over again. Then I get so rushy and buzzy that my body gets out of sync with my mind, and I begin to feel discomfort in my belly and heart. And what's even worse is that I'm not even enjoying my beautiful life experience! The precious moment is slipping by me unnoticed, until it's literally gone forever, never to be retrieved!

A wonderful way I've found to remind myself to get back on track is to think of minding my "inner speed limit." This is a concept I learned from the wonderful book *Open Heart, Open Mind* by Tsoknyi Rinpoche. Rinpoche defines the inner speed limit as "a comfortable margin of activity that allows us to complete the tasks with which we're faced on a daily basis without receiving a mental, emotional, or physical speeding ticket." So the inner speed limit isn't about doing less or about doing things at a snail's pace, it's about doing what we're doing without getting ahead of ourselves. We're going to do it anyway, so why not do it with love and our full presence of mind? It's a simple, profound concept that brings such nourishment and joy to every moment.

To illustrate the inner speed limit concept, let's consider my daily shower. When I shower while thinking, "Oh, later I've got to do this and this and this, and I've got to remember to tell so-and-so about such-and-such," my stomach ties up in knots and I experience no enjoyment of the water, the shampoo, or the soap. Plus, when the shower is over, I still didn't get anything accomplished other than the shower! If, on the other hand, I bring full presence to the shower, I feel so nourished. I revel in caring for my body and send my body loving thoughts. I breathe deeply because my thoughts aren't rushing around like crazy, so my inner organs are relaxed and nourished with oxygen. I enjoy the sound of the water, the scent of the soap, and the relaxing massage of shampoo on my scalp. Plus, when I do move forward into the rest of the day, my mind is clear and calm, and I am more aligned with the Universe and the natural flow of things so all my additional tasks are actually *more* successful and efficient, not less.

Yesterday, as I was dusting while compulsively thinking about any number of other things, I accidentally nudged a decorative fan so that it became lodged behind a heavy bookshelf. Immediately, I recognized this occurrence for what it was: an inner speeding ticket! I smiled, took a breath, and thanked my inner officer for the reminder as I brought the fullness of my present-moment awareness to the act of moving the bookshelf and retrieving the fan. Needless to say, in addition to increasing my effectiveness, revising my pace allowed me to enjoy the remainder of my cleaning day much, much more than I otherwise would have.

Conscious Consumption

Conscious alignment with the Universe and with Mother Earth naturally entails conscious consumption. When we slow down and tune into our bodies, and when we see how inextricably interconnected we are with every living thing, we naturally desire to eat healthy, life-giving foods and to make purchasing decisions that are in alignment with the best interests of the environment.

When I was twenty-one, I lived and worked for some months on the edge of the Grand Canyon. Just about every day during that time I took a walk along a trail that bordered the canyon and often sat on a ledge for an hour or so, just gazing out into the quiet depths. Also during that time, without any outside influence other than Mother Earth herself, I began naturally desiring to stop eating meat and to recycle and reuse whenever I possibly could. It wasn't because I thought I *should*, it was because I *knew* in my gut that these were the right things to do. Even after I returned from the Grand Canyon, I continued these habits for some time before they fell by the wayside, right along with the inner peace I had found by living in such proximity to the natural world. Years later, through consciously rekindling my connection, I rediscovered my inherent desire to do my very best to make decisions that were in alignment with the earth. To this day, I find that the more I cultivate my alignment with All That Is, the more I refine my consumption habits and let go of habits that don't support the planet. Through looking deeply and attuning to the wisdom within and around me, I can see that when something doesn't support the planet, it doesn't support me, and vice versa.

The bottom line is that Mother Earth is powerful! When we notice and honor our interconnection with her, we are deeply nourished by her power, and we can ride its tide as we allow it to fuel our intentions and magical workings.

Devotional Self-Care

Many of us were subtly or overtly raised with the idea that the physical body (and even the whole physical world) is somehow bad, dirty, and wrong. And even if we had very open-minded parents, we were still raised—and live—in a culture with a long philosophical tradition of shunning the realm of the body and the senses. But when you consider that everything is connected—that there is no separation between form and spirit, and that the entire physical world constantly reflects and interacts with the nonphysical—the concept of the intellect and spirit being morally superior to the body appears to possess some serious flaws. In addition to being illogical, it teaches us to distrust our sexuality and to dislike our very physical presence! Because the realm of the physical is so inherent to our very identities, as well as the survival of our species, this in turn contributes to violence and mental illness, and even lends itself to the cruel and unthinking destruction of our beautiful and life-giving earthly environment.

I mention this because when I noticed the seeds of this body-negating belief within my own consciousness and purposely released them in favor of honoring my body as the sacred vessel it is, I experienced a massive amount of healing and an enormous inflow of personal power. That's why I suggest that, as a part of your everyday magical path, you express great devotion toward your own body. Bathe it, care for it, and clothe it lovingly. Take the time to find the products that best nourish your skin and hair, and adorn yourself in the colors, textures, and patterns that feel best to you and fuel your personal power. You are a sacred being, after all; every single day, honor your physical body in the same way you might burn incense at a divine altar. Each time you do so, you'll come more and more deeply into alignment with your intuition, your magical power, Mother Earth, and All That Is.

PART 2

The Holistic Energy Magic Spellbook

Now you have a firm foundation in the elements, a working understanding of visualization and energy work, tools for living magically and consciously every day, and some solid practice under your belt. Congratulations! You're ready to work spells and rituals that will help you align with and manifest your desires. And here, in part 2, you'll find plenty of ideas for how to do just that.

If you feel that you could use one of these spells right this second, go ahead: do it. Otherwise, file it away in your mind for future use or come back to it if and when it's needed. And, of course, if you're comfortable crafting your own rituals and spells, you can use these as springboards for your own wonderful creations. Just remember to seek out the magical jolt and inspirational juice; in other words, if it feels powerful for you (provided it doesn't hurt anyone or unfairly encroach upon anyone's free will), go for it!

Chanting charms or invocations from memory (rather than from a written page) can be an extremely magical act. This is because memorizing something is a way of harmonizing yourself with its essence and making it your own. And because everything is energy and you always get out of magic what you put into it (albeit in a different form), the act of memorizing can be like an act of devotion: an offering of effort and energy to the Universe (or to the deity or being to whom you are chanting) on the same level as burning incense, singing, or lighting a candle. It's also a fun way to increase your magical repertoire, which in turn expands your magical expertise.

As noted in previous chapters, if you choose to do a ritual containing a chant or invocation and you're in a situation where you feel comfortable speaking the words aloud, please do so. Otherwise, go ahead and simply think them.

Cleansing and Clearing

PERSONAL CLEANSE: Lemon Light

A simple and lovely way to powerfully cleanse your energy field is to imagine a powerful whirlwind of bright, sparkly, light yellow, lemon-scented light swirling through and around you. See it whipping away and detoxifying all challenging and stuck energy and then cocooning you in its protective, glowing freshness.

PERSONAL CLEANSE: Breeze

In her wonderful book *Practical Protection Magick*, author Ellen Dugan suggests allowing yourself to be cleansed by the element of air by stepping outside into the breeze, holding your arms out, and letting it blow around you. As you do this, feel the air invigorating you and blowing away any and all negativity or stuck energy. And even if you're indoors or it's not windy out, you can mentally invoke the element of air and feel *as if* it's whipping around you, powerfully cleansing you in just the same way.

Cut Cords of Attachment

This ritual is designed to help you cut energetic cords of attachment between you and another person. This can be helpful when a person is not actually in your physical space but they seem to be lingering on in your mind or generally sending you less-than-desirable energy from afar. It can also be helpful when you aren't in a position to physically remove yourself from the person or relationship, but you would like to stop any and all relationship-related energy drains. I suggest following it up with a strong protective visualization of your choosing.

Stand upright and visualize yourself growing roots that anchor you in the molten core of the earth. Then extend branches high into the sky. Connect with the infinite light of the cosmos, and let your branches hang back down like a weeping willow and caress the earth once again. Say:

Mother Earth, I hereby banish and release all cords
of attachment between me and _ _ _ _.

Father Sky, I hereby banish and release all cords
of attachment between me and _ _ _ _.

All cords are severed, all cords are
demolished, all cords are destroyed.

All cords are canceled, cleared, deleted, and erased
in all directions of time, never to return.

All my energy now floods back to me, filling me with vitality
and encircling me powerfully in a protective sphere of light.

Thank you.

As you surround yourself in a sphere of visualized white
sage smoke, see any and all energetic cords of attachment
being completely deleted and destroyed. Then see any for-
merly co-opted energy returning to you as bright white
light. See this light swirl around you in a rapid clockwise spiral and then return to your energy field, giving you a boost
of vitality and surrounding you in a sphere of white light.

Guilt-Clearing Visualization

You've heard it a million times, but it bears repeating:
we all make mistakes—all of us. And while guilt can sometimes be a natural side effect of a mistake, especially when
we perceive that mistake to have negatively affected another
in some way, it never helps to hold onto it. In fact, guilt has
such a challenging and sticky vibration that it can actually
do even more harm to hang onto it than to let go of it. For
example, if you're holding onto guilt toward a family member, that guilt will constantly hover between you, casting
a shadow on your every interaction. And if you're holding
onto guilt toward a deceased loved one, that deceased loved
one may feel responsible for putting your mind at ease and
therefore may be somewhat more tethered to the physical
realm more than he or she prefers at this stage. (Be assured
that no matter how heavy and serious things may seem from

this side of the veil, from the perspective of those who have crossed over, bygones really are bygones.) The truth is, once something has happened, it's what happened. While of course asking for forgiveness and making amends is often a wise and appropriate thing to do, incessantly regretting what happened is fighting against the truth, and you will always lose that fight. It's just a waste of energy, and it holds you back from being the best you in the present moment that you can possibly be. So for everyone's sake, let yourself off that hook and let go! And if you need a little extra help, give this visualization a try.

Sit or recline with your spine straight. Close your eyes and take some deep, conscious breaths as you notice anyplace where you are holding onto tension. Breathe into that tension and let it naturally dissolve. When you feel relaxed and open, visualize yourself standing in a gently rolling field of lavender at sunset on a warm evening. Even if you've never been in a field of lavender in real life, pretend that you know exactly what it looks, feels, and smells like. Notice the flowers gently swaying in the balmy breeze. Inhale the strong, sweet, relaxing scent as it wafts around you.

In time, you notice six angels standing in front of you, glowing with an almost blindingly bright white light. These angels are holding a bag made of white light, as if they're expecting you to place something into it. You look down and notice that you're wearing a pendant on a chain around your neck. This pendant is a small bottle filled with heavy, murky liquid. It is your guilt! As you remove it from your neck, you notice that it is quite heavy—much heavier than you expected. When you throw it into the glowing white bag, you feel so much lighter than you did before. Instantly, the angels close the glowing bag around it and wordlessly communicate that they will take it up to their heavenly realm, where it will be completely dissolved and transmuted into light. And then, in a flash, they are gone. You glance up just in time to see them disappear into a cloud.

Again, notice the lavender around you and become aware that it is sentient and wise. Silently, the lavender assures you and gives you the strong feeling that you are safe and completely correct in letting go of your guilt. Emotions such as sadness or loss may remain, as these move through the psyche in their own way and time, but there is no valid reason to keep hanging onto the guilt. Inhale the scent of the lavender once more, and feel it brush your brow and your heart with energy and renewal. Revel in the lightness and feel confident in your ability to leave the past behind. You are free.

Open your eyes, flick your fingers toward the ground nine times, and then shake your hands, symbolically releasing any residual guilt into the energy of the earth.

Cleanse for Another Person

To cleanse another person's energy field of challenging or stagnant energies, you might try this visualization, which I first learned about from the teachings of author Doreen Virtue. Once you've cleansed and shielded your own energy field (as above), tune into the other person's true self on the internal plane. Then ask her: "Is it okay if I energetically cleanse you?" It's highly likely that you'll sense her saying yes in your mind's eye, either by nodding, speaking, smiling, or just giving you a feeling that it's fine for you to proceed. If you don't, however, you can explain to her that it won't hurt her at all and will only help. If she still does not seem to agree, stop and do not proceed. If she does agree, however, you can then call on archangel Michael (or a helper of your choice) to vacuum her of all challenging energies. See him doing this with a vacuum tube of light. Then ask him to surround her in a sphere of very bright white or indigo light, in which only love remains and through which only love may enter. For household harmony and everyone's general well-being, it's a good idea to do this daily for the people and animals who live in your household. You might get in the habit of doing so during your daily meditation. If you feel guided, it can also be a good idea to do this for people with whom you seem to be in conflict, such as challenging neighbors or coworkers. (Always be sure to cleanse and shield yourself first!)

Cleanse an Object

For the environment and my bank account, I often like to shop secondhand, and even when the energy of a new-to-me item feels generally positive, I still don't want to unwittingly pick up an energetic pattern that is not in alignment with my truest good. What's more, I sometimes want to cleanse the energy of a crystal but I don't want to take the time to burn sage smoke around it, run it under cold water, or set it in sunlight. If you can relate to either of these situations, or really anytime you want to instantly cleanse and reset the energy of an object, this instant ritual can help.

Simply hold or direct your palms toward the item and visualize it igniting into a ball of golden-white, extra-hot fire. See this fire burning away and transmuting all negativity into positivity and blessings. Next, send visualized white sage smoke completely through and around the item, to remove any and all lingering energetic patterns from the past. Finally, bless the item with an energetic quality of your choice, such as peace, harmony, abundance, or love. Visualize a sphere of white light around the item, spinning slowly in a clockwise direction, and send the vibration of your chosen quality through that light. For example, you might simply think the word (for example, "harmony") as you envision and focus on the rotating sphere of light. You might finish by thinking or saying a basic finalization phrase such as my favorite all-purpose standby:

Thank you, thank you, thank you. Blessed be. And so it is.

HOME CLEANSE: Invisible Smudge

Whether you're physically home or not, call up your home in your mind. In your mind's eye, see the weather as mild and sunny, with a light breeze. Open all the windows and notice the light and air streaming in. Then see yourself standing in a central location and lighting a huge bundle of dried white sage so that it's smoking like incense. See this smoke billowing into a huge cloud. Since it's magic smoke, it expands outward without you even having to move and swirls in a counterclockwise direction (to clear and disperse) into all the corners and crevices, clearing and raising the vibration of your home to a very clear degree. As the smoke continues to fill and fumigate your home of all challenging energies, call on archangel Michael to escort any and all stuck energies and earthbound entities to the light. Finally, see the smoke dissipate and envision a very bright sphere of golden-white light completely filling and surrounding the space, moving in a slight clockwise direction (to seal in the energy). Ask angels to surround your home in a circle, preserving this positive energy and protecting the space from all negativity.

HOME CLEANSE: Elements
With your eyes open or closed, say or think:

I call on the element of air to cleanse this space.

Visualize and imagine gales of wind blowing through every room and area of your home, dislodging negativity and blowing it out your windows and doors.
Then say or think:

I call on the element of fire to cleanse this space.

Visualize the roof of your house disappearing and hot desert sun searing down into every crevice of your home, powerfully disinfecting it and breaking apart any heaviness or darkness. Replace the roof.

Then say or think:

I call on the element of water to cleanse this space.

Visualize clear, gentle waves of saltwater rushing through your home, cleansing it, refreshing it, and renewing it.
Then say or think:

I call on the element of earth to cleanse this space.

Visualize the floor of your house disappearing and soft, cool, receptive clay earth absorbing and neutralizing any and all negativity. See it pulling out impurities like a healing mud mask. Replace the floor.
Then say or think:

I call on the element of spirit to bless this space.

Visualize a large swirl of clear light with rainbow sparkles spiraling in a clockwise direction completely around and through your entire home, fine-tuning it and blessing it with abundance, luck, love, and all good things.
Say or think:

Air, I thank you.

Fire, I thank you.

Water, I thank you.

Earth, I thank you.

Spirit, I thank you.

Protection and Shielding

COMMONSENSE CAVEAT: As with all protection and shielding rituals, in addition to your magical endeavors, be sure to take every possible protective measure in the physical world: lock your doors, don't walk down dark alleys at night, leave any relationship or situation that you don't feel right about, and so on.

Fiery Wall of Protection

For instant, extra-strength protection from bad vibes of any variety, ask archangel Michael or the goddess Brighid (or both) to surround you with a protective wall of fire, through which absolutely no negativity can pass. In your mind's eye, see it burning and raging with a white heat and blinding brightness. Hear the crackle and roar of the flames, and know beyond all doubt that absolutely no ill will can pass through the wall of fire. When this visualization feels strong in your mind, heartily thank Michael or Brighid. For best results, refresh this visualization at least once per day and as desired throughout the day.

Golden Sphere

A sphere of golden, cosmic light within and around you can gently dissuade negativity by harmonizing and balancing your energy while healing and sealing your aura. As an experiment, you might try this every morning for a week and see how you feel.

While sitting comfortably with your spine straight, anchor yourself into the earth by sending roots deep into her glowing core. As your roots settle into the core of the earth, feel yourself being tugged down into the floor. Comfortably settle in. When this feels complete, tune into the glittering, infinite cosmos above you. Using your inner sense, seek out a cache of golden light nestled somewhere in a pocket of space, like a vein of gold nestled in a mountain, then simply bring it down into the crown of your head.

Fill your entire body and aura with this light. Feel it neutralizing and dispersing negativity, weaving together all the parts of your aura, filling in any dark areas or holes, and generally bringing you into harmonious balance. See yourself cocooned in a sphere of shiny gold light that is impervious to negativity or harm. Thank the earth and cosmos. Repeat once per day or as desired.

Pink Bubble of Light

If for any reason you feel compelled to be present at a gathering or situation that may not be physically dangerous but rather may be draining, awkward, painful, or generally unbearable, you might try surrounding yourself in a soft, sweet bubble of pink light to help you coast above the discord and energetically soften any harshness before it reaches you. Imagine the light and set the intention to remain happy and at peace. Then you might fortify your intention with the following chant (to be said inwardly or aloud):

> *Guardian angels and all angels bright*
> *Surround me in a rosy light*
> *Through this day I'll softly flow*
> *Protected in this sugared glow.*

Deflect Negativity from a Particular Source

For this ritual, while you don't need to have a black tourmaline on hand, it is necessary to have a firsthand familiarity with its energetic and metaphysical properties. Just reading about them won't do it, but you could go spend some quality time with a black tourmaline in a store without actually buying it. However, actually having spent some consecutive days and nights with the stone before you ever need to perform this ritual is ideal.

If you suspect or know that someone specific is sending you some bad vibes (in the form of negative thoughts or wishes, or even magic performed out of ill will) and you feel that it's negatively affecting your life, surround yourself in a shroud of black tourmaline: in other words, send its energy all throughout your body and aura. See this lightly shining, pitch-black energy encircle you in a sphere, immediately absorbing and neutralizing any and all negative effects of being on the receiving end of this person's projections. Notice that this takes the pressure off and gives you more of a sense of relaxation, like the whole thing is not actually that big of a deal. Also, feel and sense that any additional energy sent toward you simply loses momentum, releases its energetic charge, stops, and slides down the sides of this sphere of energy and into the earth without ever entering your aura at all. (It's sort of like you have no bars on your cell phone: you're no longer receiving a signal because you're officially off the grid!) Finish by surrounding and filling yourself with a sphere of very bright white light.

EXTRA STRENGTH: Deflect Negativity from a Particular Source

This somewhat intense ritual is appropriate for somewhat intense situations. For example, if you feel strongly that you are receiving negative energy or spiritual ill will from a particular person or group of people, and it's gotten to a point where you feel you could use some extra strength deflecting, you might want to perform this ritual as a form of proactive magical first aid. Please note, however, that it's very rare that you'll receive this amount of intentional negativity from a person or group, although it can happen. If it's happened to you, don't panic (never, *ever* panic): remember that you're a very powerful spiritual being with the absolute ability to determine what energy is and is not allowed to affect you and your life experience.

Go outside to a natural and secluded setting that feels especially cleansing and rejuvenating to you. A secluded area of a city park or a park with relatively few visitors is okay in a pinch. Stand with your feet on grass, dirt, or sand—ideally barefoot—and feel the comforting, reassuring solidity of Mother Earth beneath your feet. Connect with the sky and see cosmic light flow down from above and cocoon you in a sphere of protective energy. Now imagine a whirlpool of positive earth/cosmic light swirling counterclockwise through the sphere that is your entire body and energy field, using centrifugal force to fling out any negative patterns of energy that you may have absorbed. See these patterns exiting your energy field and falling into the earth to be reabsorbed, composted, and detoxified.

Once you feel that any challenging patterns have left your energy field, hold your hands up over your head, palms facing out to the sides. Imagine your palms powerfully deflecting any additional incoming negativity like mirrors deflecting sunlight. Stamp your right foot forcefully and say:

Now and in the future, I absolutely refuse to absorb energy patterns that are not of my choosing.

I now banish, cast out, and powerfully deflect all that does not serve me.

In the name of earth, air, fire, water, and spirit,
I now deflect all that does not serve me.

In the name of the God and Goddess,
I now deflect all that does not serve me.

I am the master of myself, I am the master of
my life, I am the master of my domain.

Thank you, earth; thank you, air; thank you, fire;
thank you, spirit; thank you, God and Goddess.

Thank you, thank you, thank you. Blessed be. And so it is.

Lower your arms and feel nothing but positive energy
swirling around you, cocooning and powerfully protecting
you. Feel confident that your ritual has succeeded, and in
the days and weeks ahead, systematically replace all fear and
worry with confidence and comfort, calling on the God and
Goddess as desired.

Banish a Person

Every now and again, there may be a time when you
honestly need to banish someone from your property, your
neighborhood, or your life. Please note this important
caveat: because this spell does, in fact, interfere with free
will, be aware that it's simply not an option if you merely
dislike someone or wish that they wouldn't hang around
(even if you really, really, really dislike them). It's only an
option if this person is interfering with your free will to

feel safe and happy, and you feel that you have absolutely no physical-world options for effectively removing them from your life and protecting your space from their presence.

Just to be on the safe side, if there's any question, I suggest cutting the cords first (see "Cut Cords of Attachment" in previous section) to see if you get a desired result from a less forceful spell.

One more caveat: do this with utter neutrality. If you have to lean one way or the other, lean toward wishing this person well. There is no need to add aggression or anger to this ritual; indeed, it will only complicate the energy and could cause unpleasant problems for you down the line (believe me, you don't want this; I learned this one the hard way). Remember that your objective is to banish this person from your life: nothing more, nothing less. Don't worry: there'll be plenty of time to feel angry later when you're *not* working magic!

Go to a moving body of water or a crossroads that is secluded and at least somewhat distant from your property and all areas where you spend the bulk of your days.

Facing the center of the crossroads or the moving body of water, hold your hands together in a cup, away from your body, as if you are holding sand. Visualize a sphere composed of dried sticks hovering a few inches above your hands, interwoven with at least one visualized hair from the head of the person you wish to banish (you might visualize yourself plucking it from her head as she sleeps). Say:

This sphere represents _ _ _ _
(full name of the person you want to banish).

Visualize this sphere catching fire. Hear the flames crackling and feel the heat on your face as you say:

I now cleanse all traces of this person from my life.

See this sphere turn to ash (while still hovering over your hands in the shape of a bubble) and visualize interspersing it with cleansing sea salt. Say:

I now banish all traces of this person from my life.

Blow the invisible sphere of ashes and salt out of your hands and toward the water or the center of the crossroads. Visualize and feel a gust of wind coming up from behind you just as you blow, helping to powerfully disperse the ball of ashes in the direction you are blowing them. As you imagine this energy dispersing to the winds and being broken up and washed away by the water or the moving energy of the crossroads, say:

> *I banish you from my home.*
> *I banish you from my work.*
> *I banish you from my family.*
> *I banish you from my life.*
> *Where I go, you shall not enter.*
> *It shall be as if you live in a distant country.*
> *It shall be as if you are on the other side of the world.*

Wipe your hands together as if you're cleaning your hands of this person. Then shake your hands off as if you're drying them at the same moment that you feel an additional gust of wind rush around you toward the water or the center of the crossroads, completely and powerfully purifying all the final traces of this person's energy from you. Instantly turn around, walk away, and don't look back.

When you get home, follow up with a cleansing ritual and then a protective ritual of your choice. A desired change should occur within one or two weeks.

Home Protection

After performing a cleansing ritual or visualization for your home, or anytime you'd like an extra boost of confident protection for your space, ask for a circle of angels to completely surround your home, facing inward. Ask them to preserve and protect all positivity within.

Then ask for another circle of angels to surround the first circle of angels, facing out. Request that this circle of angels protect your home from any and all incoming negativity. Ask that they neutralize it, disperse it, or direct it back to its source.

Finally, envision your home completely surrounded by a giant energetic tree trunk. See the roots of this tree reaching deep into the earth and the branches of this tree stretching high into the sky. Ask this tree to draw up soothing, harmonizing earth energy and draw down invigorating, beautifying cosmic energy. Your home is now protected on all sides, as well as above and below. Thank the angels and the tree.

Divine Mother Magic

Whether you're male or female, and whether you have children or you don't, you have a deep relationship with the Divine Mother, and you powerfully possess her archetype within you. The following rituals have to do with divinely maternal intentions, which include intentions related to parenting but also to healing, family harmony, and living with an open and compassionate heart.

Moon Star Sun Blessing (to Protect a Child)

Calling on the Lord and Lady—specifically the primordial Divine Feminine and Divine Masculine in their roles as mother and father—is an excellent way to protect your child in mind, body, and spirit. (But of course, as always, also take every precaution in the physical world!) This spoken charm will do just that. Remember: as you speak the words, bring their essences and visuals into your mind and intentionally direct them into the energy of your ritual.

Whisper the following outside the door of your child's room as he or she sleeps, say it in your mind as you hold him, or (if he is not in your vicinity) call him to mind and see yourself whispering or saying this over him:

Mother and Father who watch over all,
Please place a moon on this child's brow.
May it deflect all that is not love.
May it guard him from all harm.

Mother and Father who watch over all,
Please place a blue star above his head.
May it guide him away from danger.
May it keep him on the path that is safe.

Mother and Father who watch over all,
Please place sunshine in his heart.
May it shine in freedom, may it blaze in courage.
May it keep him always in the light of your love.

Thank you.

Divine Mother Charm to Soothe a Child

While holding a crying child, say or think the following words gently while feeling them from your heart and envisioning the essences of what they name:

Divine Mother with heart of rose quartz,
Divine Mother with essence of white feathers,

Divine Mother with womb that heals the world,
Because you are here, this child is soothed.

This child is soothed yesterday.
This child is soothed today.
This child is soothed tomorrow.

Before this child is love, behind this child is love.
To the left and to the right of this child is love.
Above this child is love, below this child is love.
Within this child is love.

A deep calm abides.
A deep trust abides.
A deep happiness abides.

Divine Mother, I thank you.
Divine Mother, I thank you.
Divine Mother, I thank you.

Inner Child Healing Visualization

If you were emotionally wounded as a child and you haven't done any work on healing your inner child, chances are your relationships and life situation are suffering for it. For example, you might feel unable to trust others, you might experience creative stagnation, or you might find yourself repeatedly making decisions that obviously don't serve you. Healing the inner child doesn't happen in one fell swoop, but this ritual can help you make contact and begin to recover the personal power that has been co-opted by the pain of the past. And if you repeat the ritual over time, your inner child *can* heal, and you can make amazing break-throughs in numerous areas of your life.

Sit or lie comfortably. Place your left hand on your heart and your right hand on your lower belly. Close your eyes, take some conscious breaths, and allow your body to relax. Now, get a sense of the Divine Mother archetype. The Divine Mother is totally loving and accepting of all her children, including you. Whether or not you had a positive relationship with your earthly mother, your Divine Mother is there for you, totally supporting and cradling you. Many incarnations of the Divine Mother are associated with roses and the sea, so you might hear the sound of the ocean or smell the scent of roses to get in alignment with her energy.

Once you feel that you've brought her into your conscious mind, say:

> *Divine Mother, be with me.*
> *Divine Mother, enter me.*

Now feel/sense/imagine the Divine Mother stepping into your physical body, merging with your essence, and awakening her wisdom within you. Now that you feel that you've merged with her essence, allow yourself to be open to your inner child. Allow yourself to see or sense your younger self at whatever age you naturally appear.

Then notice what your younger self is feeling and doing. Is she crying? Laughing? Dancing? Hiding? Just like a loving parental figure, interact with her in the way that will most comfort and nourish her. If she's open to it, ask her what she needs. She might ask for a hug or for you to listen or for you to allow her to play more often. The important thing is that you assure her that you are strong and capable, and that you can take care of her in exactly the way she needs.

When this feels complete, recognize that your inner child is always present within you. Ask the Divine Mother to help you have a healthy relationship with your inner child and support her in every way you can. Then thank the Divine Mother and open your eyes. Now, consider what you've learned and see if there are any changes that you can make in your adult life to help make your inner child feel more loved and valuable. For example, perhaps you can set aside a little time every week to dance, play in the garden, watch cartoons, or do crafts.

Create a Healing Environment

If you or someone you know is convalescing, ask archangel Michael to vacuum the healing room of all challenging energies, and then ask archangel Raphael to fill the space with a clean emerald-green crystalline light. Then ask archangel Michael to bless four etheric white quartz points with the energy of purity, protection, and positivity, and mentally place them in the four corners of the room, pointing in. Charge these invisible crystals with the intention to preserve the pure vibration and vibrant healing energy within the space.

Gardenia Distance Healing

Gardenia blossoms possess a very purifying, loving, healing vibration. As such, to send healing energy from a distance to someone in need, surround him or her, in your mind's eye, with a giant gardenia blossom. Also visualize a halo of smaller gardenia blossoms completely surrounding the patient, remembering to visualize the scent as well as the image. Once this is clear in your mind, let it go. Then, whenever this person or animal happens to pop into your mind throughout the day, refresh the visualization. Continue until he or she is healed or at least sufficiently on the road to recovery.

Hands-On Healing

Many hands-on healing modalities, such as Reiki and craniosacral therapy, require no physical tools. Similarly, you can send healing energy through your hands—to yourself or another—in the following way.

Visualize your connection with the earth. Send roots deep into the core, and draw golden-white earth energy up from below. Then visualize your connection with the cosmos. Send branches far out into outer space, and draw sparkling rainbow light down from above. See these energies merge at your heart center and flow out your arms and through the palms of your hands. Place your hands on or near the person who needs healing, wherever you feel drawn to place them (obviously without violating their personal space against their will). Feel yourself directing this golden-white/rainbow light into the person's body and energy field.

Know and trust that this light knows exactly what to do: what to clear, what to bolster, and what to shift. Move your hands as you feel guided, and continue until you feel that the healing session is complete.

You can also do this to parts of your own body that need healing.

Sacred Grove Charm for Family Harmony

A thriving grove of trees is a strong metaphor for a happy and harmonious family. Prepare for this ritual by clearing yourself, clearing each member of the family or household, and clearing the energy of your home. Then, from a relaxed and grounded place, holding every family member in your heart with love and without judgment, say:

A sacred grove, our roots go deep,
As the wheel turns, our love doth keep.

Vital one and vital all,
Though we may bend, we'll never fall.

As peace and joy both circle round,
Our sacred grove is sacred bound.

Quan Yin Alignment for Sensitive Souls

Sensitive, compassionate, empathic people sometimes feel overwhelmed by turning on the news or simply contemplating any aspect of the cruelty, sadness, and struggle perpetuated and experienced by our fellow earthlings. Indeed, sometimes it seems the more conscious and energetically open we get, the more open we are to the waves of heart-break that appear to characterize this life experience. This can be especially confusing because, at the same time, our sensitivity allows us to see that the more positivity and joy we can muster, the more healing we will bring to the world.

This practice aligns us with the Quan Yin Consciousness, a grid of energy that constantly surrounds the earth with compassion and love. (Some call it the Christ Consciousness and prefer to associate it with Jesus Christ, but it also may be accurately named after any purely compassionate ascended master with whom you resonate, such as Saint Francis, Mary Magdalene, or Krishna.) This can be a great blessing to those of us who have chosen to be open-hearted warriors: beings who witness horror and injustice while also being beacons and cheerleaders of love, forgiveness, and positivity in order to help shift things for the better.

I suggest performing this alignment every day as needed, just before bed, first thing in the morning, or as a part of your daily meditation. But first, relax and envision very bright pinkish-white light bathing, repairing, restructuring, and strengthening your heart, and then expanding through-out your entire body and aura.

With your eyes closed and your hands resting open on your knees or thighs, index fingers and thumb tips lightly touching, inhale deeply and think:

Consciousness, expand to the Quan Yin Consciousness.

Then, with pursed lips, exhale, sending your awareness and energy field to connect with the Quan Yin Consciousness, which you may perceive in your mind's eye as a geometrical grid of pinkish-white light that surrounds and hovers above the earth from the level of the heart (about three to four feet off the ground) to about the level of a four-story building.

Now that you're plugged into this energy, consider the deep meaning of Quan Yin's moniker, "The Bodhisattva of Infinite Compassion." As a being who chooses to stay present on earth until all beings realize enlightenment and know peace, she is an excellent spiritual ally for times when we feel overwhelmed by the human challenges and heartbreak of the planet, as she reminds us to be loving and compassionate with ourselves and also with every other single being on earth.

Take a moment to request that Quan Yin support your efforts to keep your heart open while also bringing courage, blessings, love, healing, and vibrant positivity to the planet. Request the ability to relentlessly love everyone and everything fully, unconditionally, and with deep compassion. Then notice the grid of light encircling the earth remaining as an identical grid splits off from it and begins to shrink in size while retaining its full potency. Keep your awareness on this shrinking grid until it reaches the size of a large grapefruit and resides around your heart, protecting and bolstering it while allowing it to stay open, receptive, and compassionate.

Heartlight Blessing for Mother Earth and All Her Inhabitants

Consider that a single strand of DNA contains the blueprint to the organism in its entirety. Similarly, one single human heart, when ignited with love, possesses the key to restoring love and wholeness to the entire planet. Indeed, those of us who are spiritually tuned in usually feel an emptiness or an excess of ungrounded energy when we do not take at least a little bit of time each day to bless and send love to our Mother Earth and all her inhabitants.

Consider performing this daily at a time that works for you: for example, you might get in the habit of doing it after yoga, before dinner, as a part of your daily attunement practice, or just before bed. The light at your heart is very powerful, so making this a regular habit will bring great benefits to the world. As an added bonus, it will help increase your personal vitality, happiness, and abundance.

Sit comfortably, with your spine straight. Close your eyes, relax, and take some deep breaths. Place your right hand over your heart, and your left hand over right hand. Envision very bright pink light at your heart as you bring to mind the animals of the world, perhaps starting with one or two animals that you have a personal, loving relationship with. Think or say:

> *I send love to all animals. All animals that fly, all animals that crawl, all animals that swim, all animals that walk. I send love to animals who are imprisoned and animals who are free.*

Open your palms outward and send the pink light throughout the globe to all animals.

Place your hands on your heart again, and envision very bright white light as you bring to mind the humans of the world, letting one or two humans that you particularly love float into your mind first in order to open your heart as fully as possible. Think or say:

> *I send love to all humans: humans who are young, humans who are middle aged, and humans who are old. Humans of every nationality and on every continent. Humans who have much, humans who have little, and everyone in between.*

Open your palms outward and send the white light throughout the globe to all humans.

Place your hands on your heart again. Envision very bright blue light at your heart as you bring to mind a wild location particularly near and dear to your heart, and then the rocks, soil, water, and air of the entire world. Think or say:

> *I send love to the ball of soil and rock that is the planet, and the water that runs through it, as well as the atmosphere that surrounds it. I send love to the deserts, mountains, forests, meadows, oceans, rivers, lakes, and ponds. I send love to the earth on which I sit and the air that I breathe.*

Open your palms outward and send the blue light throughout the globe to the globe itself.

Place your hands on your heart again. Envision very bright emerald-green light as you bring to mind a tree or plant that you particularly feel aligned with, and then the green and growing things of the world. Think or say:

I send love to all the green and growing things. I send love to the plants that grow underwater and the plants that grow in open air. I send love to cultivated plants and wild ones. I send love to plants that live indoors and plants that live outdoors. I send love to all the flowers, weeds, trees, herbs, and shrubs of the world.

Open your palms outward and send the green light throughout the globe to all plants.

Place your hands on your heart again. Visualize emerald-green light once more as you bring to mind your own heart center, the heart of the planet, and the heart of every living being. Think or say:

I send love to my own heart. I send love to the heart of the planet. I send love to the hearts of all people and animals on the planet. May we all be blessed with health, happiness, vitality, and abundance. Thank you.

Portal of Light Visualization to Support a Transitioning Loved One

We live in a culture that seems to feel really great about the transition of energy known as birth but really terrible about the transition of energy known as death, although just like birth, *everyone* is destined to experience it. Also, just like birth, although the actual transition may be painful and scary, it is a natural and beautiful shift from one form of consciousness to another.

As someone who has chosen to deeply tune into the energetic reality of this life experience, you have the rare ability to be someone who can stay present with a transitioning loved one, rather than succumbing to the all-too-common practice of avoiding or denying the situation in any number of ways. And staying present with a transitioning loved one—human or otherwise—is such a gift! It's a gift to the loved one, as they feel your courage and love with them until the very end of this current life experience, but it's also a gift to you. Being open and awake with someone as they round the bend and move beyond the veil is a transcendent experience, and one that reminds us of both the fleeting preciousness of life and the eternal nature of our souls.

If you have the ability to be present when the actual transition occurs, relax and stay as grounded, brave, and open as possible. Just before, during, and after, visualize a portal of very bright white light encompassing the loved one. Send visualized sweetgrass smoke throughout this portal, further opening up the veil between the worlds and urging your loved one to ascend and move out of this physical dimension in the best and most pleasant of ways. See your loved one on the soul level, completely dissolving into light.

Magic for Our Animal Friends

Saint Francis Animal Protection

Saint Francis was a gentle saint who lived in harsh times. Despite (or, more accurately, because of) this gentleness, Saint Francis is an extremely strong protector. He protects through surrounding your beloved pets in a strong cocoon of loving intentions. Since like attracts like, this strongly dissuades threats of all kinds from entering the energy field of your animal friend, keeping her wrapped in an energetic swaddling of safety and positivity.

To invoke this protection, hold your hands in a heart-calming mudra: left hand cradled in right, palms up, thumb tips touching, pinkie-side of hands resting near bellybutton.

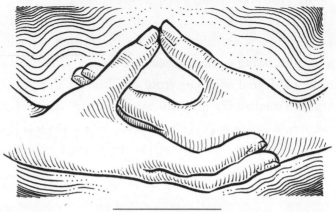

Heart-Calming Mudra

As you envision your animal surrounded in a protective bubble of warmth and light, say or think:

Saint Francis of Assisi, beloved friend to all creatures,

Thank you for powerfully protecting _ _ _ _ from all harm.

Thank you for surrounding her in light.

Thank you for surrounding her in love.

Thank you for surrounding her in compassion.

Thank you for guiding her in safety

And protecting her from harm.

For this kindness, and for all your kindnesses,

I thank you.

Saint Francis General Animal Blessing

If you have one or more animal friends of any kind whom you'd like to bless with all good things, perform this ritual.

While standing upright, close your eyes and hold your arms at 30-degree angles up from your sides, palms facing forward. Visualize the peaceful Saint Francis giving a sermon to the birds or hugging his donkey. When you feel that you've made contact with his essence, say or think:

Saint Francis of Assisi, you who love and desire
The very best for all animals, I call on you.
Please bless the animals of this place [or insert
your animal's name here] with love.

Please bless them with health.
Please bless them with happiness.
Please bless them with harmony.

When they communicate, may they be understood.
When they are understood, may their wishes be honored.

May peace prevail for them and all animals
Now and in all directions of time. Thank you.

Feel the saint's sincere appreciation for your heartfelt desire to serve animals and make life better for them. With a loving smile, see him accepting your request and then sense him sending a generous helping of blessings and light toward your dear animal friends.

Bast Protection for the Independent Cat

If you have a cat who goes outside and disappears all day, if you're worried because the cat ran out the door against your wishes or decided to stay out all night, or even if you have an indoor cat that you're leaving alone for a few days, perhaps you'd like to invoke the truly fierce protection of Her Royal Highness, the Egyptian cat goddess and matron of independent cats everywhere, Bast.

To do so, kneel on the floor and place your hands on your thighs, palms up. Close your eyes and imagine yourself alone in an ancient temple that smells of sweet incense and oils. This is the temple of Bast. Say or think:

Bast, I call on you.

Bast, I call on you.

Bast, I call on you.

Slowly, begin to notice a deep and resonant purr that soothes and massages you from the inside out, filling the entire temple. This is Bast's presence. Envision her as a very large cat seated on her haunches before you on a raised dais, with her front legs straight. As she gazes at you, you can sense her fierce protectiveness. Even though her face is impassive, you still get a strong sense of her natural, maternal love and support for all felines everywhere. Say or think:

Bast, I am devoted to my cat _____, and it is my sacred pledge
to love, adore, and care for her for all the days of her life. Today,
I ask that you watch over her and keep her safe from all harm.

For this protection of ___ ___ ___ ___, I thank you and honor you.
For your protection of cats everywhere, I thank you
and honor you. For your regal and resplendent beauty
that blesses the world, I thank you and honor you.

Inwardly sense Bast agreeing to protect your beloved cat as she gazes at you with her golden eyes and royally inclines her head ever so slightly. Relax as you realize that your cat is perfectly safe in the care of this fierce and loving goddess. (Although do realize that Bast fully expects you to continue to do everything in your power to protect your cat as well.)

A Blessing for the Animals Who Suffer at the Hands of Humans

My dear friend Rachel and I recently planned and performed this animal blessing ritual together. If you choose to perform it (alone or with a partner or group), your aims will be threefold and will concentrate equally on the past, present, and future. First, you'll ask forgiveness of the animals that you and your species have harmed or contributed to the harming of in the past. Second, you'll send comfort and love to those animals who are currently suffering at the hands of humans. Third, you'll send a beam of awakening that will help energetically shift human action toward greater kindness and human consciousness toward a greater awareness of the equality of all species.

After relaxing and centering your mind, call on the Divine in a way that feels powerful for you. For example, you might simply say:

I now call on God/Goddess/All That Is to be
present and to assist me with this blessing.

Then concentrate at your heart center, and visualize a very bright sphere of cleansing white light at your heart. Bring to mind all the centuries of animals who have suffered at the hands of humans, right up until the recent past. Then, from your heart, speak words of apology on behalf of yourself and the entire human race. You might speak for a while, apologizing for specific actions and injustices, or you might simply say something like:

> *Animals who have suffered in the past at the hands*
> *of humans, I'm so sorry, on behalf of myself and my*
> *species. Please forgive me. Please forgive us.*

See the white light at your heart expand exponentially, cleansing and purifying the past, and transmuting both suffering and guilt into love.

Next, visualize a sphere of loving, comforting pink light residing at your heart. Bring to mind the animals in the present moment who are suffering at the hands of humans: in labs, slaughterhouses, factory farms, circuses, amusement parks, and everywhere else. Again speak words from your heart, invoking as much comfort and mercy as possible. Say whatever is true for you for as long as you desire, or perhaps just say something simple, like:

I invoke divine comfort and love for all animals currently
suffering at the hands of humans. God, Goddess, All That Is,
please intervene on behalf of all suffering animals, bringing them
as much peace, joy, comfort, and love as possible. Thank you.

Now see the pink light at your heart expanding outward to envelop and immerse all suffering animals in divine comfort and love.

Now, see a sphere of bright periwinkle-blue light residing at your heart center. Bring to mind the humans and animals of the present and future, and conjure up the deep inner knowing that greater consciousness and compassion can be present now and in the future, so that humans no longer overpower and exploit animals for their own amusement, appetite, or personal gain. Feel your own sense of compassion, and be aware that consciousness is highly contagious. Then powerfully set the intention to infect everyone with your perspective of kindness and equality. Now send that periwinkle light outward across the planet like a high-powered radio wave of enlightenment moving out in all directions.

Throw your hands up in the air and flick your palms outward (as if you're flinging petals to the sky) to release any residual energy and to symbolically demonstrate your intention to send loving energy throughout the planet.

Finish by addressing the Divine as you say:

Thank you, thank you, thank you. Blessed be. And so it is.

Saint Francis Charm to Help Find a Missing Animal

It's heartbreaking to see a flyer for someone's missing animal friend, but you no longer have to suffer helplessly. Next time you see one—or if you happen to have been separated from your *own* animal friend—you can enlist Saint Francis's powerful assistance and protection with the following charm.

Visualize the animal's face, inwardly state his or her name (if you know it), mentally bathe the animal in light, and think:

> Saint Francis of great light and love,
> Please gaze down from up high above.
> Find this animal from far or near,
> And unite him with what he holds dear.
> By Sister Moon and Brother Sun,
> May this be best for everyone.

Then simply thank Saint Francis from the bottom of your heart and release worry as much as possible, with the knowing that you've summoned a powerful ally to the task. (And if it's your animal friend who's lost, also be sure to do everything you can to find him or her in the physical world!)

Ally with the Wild Birds

In times past, it was common practice in some European countries to leave milk or bread out near the front door "for the fairies," to curry their favor and enlist their magical support. Similarly, I like to keep a small birdbath and scatter birdseed daily around the area of my front door for the sparrows that live nearby. Each time I scatter the birdseed, I am aware of the invisible web of energy of which I am a part. I see myself sending out energy in the form of sustenance and positive wishes for the well-being of the birds, and I know that—because whatever you send out always comes back to you in some form—I will most definitely experience blessings of abundance and positivity in return.

Birds are wild spirits of the air element, and therefore the literal and symbolic emissaries of creativity, freedom, and new beginnings, so you can inwardly request that they support you in these areas as you offer them the gift of food. Not to mention, by nourishing the wildlife in your immediate vicinity, you're increasing the beneficial chi, or life force energy, which is the same exact life force energy that flows into your home and life. From another angle, the simple presence of birds chirping and flying around happily cleanses, blesses, beautifies, and activates the area around your home, and therefore—because your home mirrors your life and vice versa—every area of your life.

Clarity and Serenity

Quan Yin Cooling Breath

Anytime you need to summon serenity, begin to notice your breath as it goes in and out. As you're doing this, inwardly call on Quan Yin, the bodhisattva of infinite compassion, and feel her settle into your body, reminding you that all is well. Once your breath naturally begins to deepen, inhale lightly and deeply through your nose, conjuring up the scent of fresh peppermint or eucalyptus as you do so. Each time you inhale this cooling air, think the word *serenity*.

As you exhale, purse your lips into a tiny O shape, as if you are blowing bubbles. As you do so, feel that you are blowing tension and worry out of your body. Each time you exhale, think the word *peace*.

Continue until you feel sufficiently serene. Finish by thinking *Quan Yin, I thank you.*

The Sun Is at My Brow: An Instant Ritual to Clear and Focus the Mind

This instant ritual can be done in public or private. (If anyone notices, it will just look like you're trying to remember something.) Whip it out before a test, a work project that requires focus, or anytime you could benefit from clearing and focusing your mind.

Close your eyes and tilt your head slightly down as you touch your third eye center (the area at the center of your forehead, about a centimeter above the area between your eyebrows) with the index finger of your right hand. Concentrate your attention on this energy center as you visualize a tiny little blindingly bright sunshine residing there as a point of utter clarity and focus. When this vision is strong and clear, inwardly chant:

The sun is at my brow,
The sun is at my brow,
The sun is at my brow.

Know that the sunshine you have invoked at your third eye center will behave like a laser beam of clarity, knowingness, and alertness, then open your eyes and proceed with the task at hand.

Get Clarity on a Major Life Decision or Find Your Life Path

Are you obsessing over a major life decision or about finding your life path? Don't! The deep, eternal aspect of you—the part of you that is one with everything—knows just what to do. What's more, the part of you that is one with everything knows that you don't have to see the whole future clearly in order to see the most immediate next step. So this ritual is about releasing your attachment to the desire to know all aspects of the distant future while getting clear on and surrendering to what feels true and right for you in this very moment.

Simply stop what you are doing, relax comfortably, and take some deep breaths. You can keep your eyes open or you can close them—whatever feels best to you. Become aware of the way that divine, infinite wisdom contains and is contained within all things. Truly, it is everywhere right now, including within you and all around you. Imagine, feel, and know the Divine as this potent, invisible wisdom that quietly permeates and defines the entire Universe all the time.

Become aware of all the tension and worry in your mind, body, and emotions as you inhale deeply. Then exhale, blowing it out and releasing it to the divine wisdom that is everywhere. Trust that you no longer have to hang onto it, because the Divine—the infinite aspect of you—is much better equipped to make the decision anyway. Continue to acknowledge your tension and obsessive thoughts and feelings as you breathe in; exhale it out to the Universe until you feel that you've let go. Then continue with your daily activities in peace, with absolute trust that you will know just what to do at exactly the time you need to know it.

In the hours and days to follow, be patient and feel safe and secure about your future, while at the same time paying very close attention to the thoughts and possibilities that bring you the greatest sense of joy and happy anticipation. That's your divine wisdom nudging you in the direction that will serve you best.

Meeting with a Helper

To receive deep insight into any issue or challenge under the sun, you might want to arrange for a little inner meeting with one of your unseen helpers, such as an angel, deity, ascended master, or deceased loved one. You might find that there's one helper in particular you like to consult, or you might switch it up according to your situation. Or you might leave it up to the helpers to decide who wants to step forward and counsel you. The following practice describes the latter option, although feel free to adapt it if you know exactly with whom you would like to consult.

Here's how you might do it:

Close your eyes and notice your breath as it goes in and out. Consciously relax your muscles, release your tension, and allow the floor or chair beneath you to fully support and cradle you. Now imagine that you are sitting in a beautiful, nourishing, comfortable space: it could be a cushioned temple, a meadow, or anywhere else that feels right. Although you appear to be alone, you clearly perceive a wise, alert presence to be there also. You can sense that this presence loves you deeply and wants to help. Now, in your mind's eye, state your challenge or question, and ask for guidance in an authentic, heartfelt way. Notice who appears before you. You may recognize this helper (or group of helpers) or you may not. Feel the loving presence of this helper, and listen deeply to what he or she has to tell you. While you may perceive actual words, you may also receive the wisdom as a thought, feeling, or energy healing. Feel free to ask additional questions as needed. Then thank the helper from the bottom of your heart, possibly offering him or her a visualized gift, such as flowers or incense, and open your eyes.

Meeting with Another Person's True Self

If you're in conflict with someone, it can be helpful to meet with his or her true self. This can give you deeper insight and understanding into the other person and can open your heart to love. This ritual draws upon the knowing that on one level, there is the illusion of discord—but on another level, both you and the other person are perfectly healthy, whole, healed, harmonious, wise, and divine. In fact, you are one.

Close your eyes and relax. Let your breath deepen naturally as you relax any areas of tension. Now make the decision to enter into the divine part of yourself: the part of you that is eternal and knows that there is no separation between you and anyone else. Feel elevated to a high point in the sky—perhaps on the top of the tallest mountain—where you can look down at the earth and see the whole picture clearly. Once this feels very clear and real to you, decide to connect with the true self of the person with whom you are experiencing a challenge. See this person in their most natural state. For example, if she loves gardening, perhaps you will see her in the most beautiful garden in the world, feeling the sunlight on her face and inhaling the fresh smell of the soil. Or if he loves flying, perhaps you see him soaring through the sky in an antique plane. You may be surprised by what you see—for example, perhaps a person who is usually dressed very plainly is transformed into a dancing gypsy. This true self is the person without any externally imposed restrictions and without the effects of harsh judgments or pain. In other words, you are seeing this person as if he or she were expressing his or her most joyful, complete self. Don't judge this or guide it with your literal mind—let it be how it appears.

When this feels real to you and you've gotten a deep sense of who this person really is, notice how happy you feel for this person and how your heart naturally opens to them. Let your true self meet with her true self and know that this is the real truth: the divine truth outside of the illusion of time and separation. Stay here for as long as feels right, and then open your eyes.

Even though you probably didn't receive clear guidance about how to proceed with regards to your seeming conflict with this person, know that you have made great strides in healing and bridging the gap between you. As Mary Magdalene says in Doreen Virtue's Goddess Guidance Deck, "Where you dwell in consciousness is where you dwell in truth."

Get Really Grounded

In chapter 2, you learned how to align with the earth element and to connect with the deep core of Mother Earth.

But if you need some extra grounding—if your thoughts are all over the place, you're full of anxiety, or you just don't feel like you're comfortably inhabiting your body—you might like to perform this movement ritual.

When you're alone, put on some really sensual, sexy music that makes your body want to move. Slip on some comfortable clothing that feels great against your skin, then slowly begin to move in a way that feels good to you. Bypass your mind and tune into your body. Don't move a single muscle unless your body wants to. If your body just wants to lie down, just lie down. If your body just wants to stretch or pet the carpet or walk slowly in a circle or shake your hips, do that.

Take at least ten minutes to let your body be the boss, and stay awake to how it shifts and changes its desires. Notice how your skin feels. Listen to the sound of the music. Inhale the scent of the room. Feel the weight of your body pressing against the floor. Open up your senses. Inhabit the present moment. Inhabit yourself.

Find Your Voice

If you need help with speaking up, speaking your truth, or even just knowing what it is you want to say or how you want to express yourself in the world, sing—loudly! If you're in the habit of hiding or apologizing for your singing voice, or if singing just plain sounds like a terrible idea, those are even more reasons to sing! At least at first, it's best to sing while you're alone. Find chanting recordings you'd like to sing along with, sing along with loud and proud songs you really like, or just sing any cheerful, angry, or boisterous song you can think of. (I don't recommend soft and sweet songs for this exercise.) Continue for at least ten minutes, but possibly more. If you're in an apartment or share your space with others, you can do this in your car.

Water Gazing

To gain clarity on any issue, you might perform this ritual as an alternative to physical divination tools like runes, tarot cards, or the I Ching. Simply relax, close your eyes, and visualize yourself on the edge of a pond in moonlight, gazing at the still surface of the water. When your mind feels still and your heart feels calm, ask your question.

Just like with physical divination tools, rather than asking yes or no questions, it's ideal to ask something open ended like "Please give me insight into ____" or "What guidance will help me with ____?"

Continuing to gaze at the water, notice what images appear in the depths. Don't impose your expectations on them, and don't try to make sense out of them just yet. For now, let them be what they are. If you need a little extra help on how to do this, imagine how you feel when a song ends on the radio and another one is about to start: your mind is simply relaxed and expectant but not attached.

Perhaps you'll see one image or perhaps you'll see several. They might shift and move or they might stay static. Just pay attention. Once the pictures stop, or if they keep repeating, open your eyes. Allow yourself to apply what you've seen to your question. If you can't seem to make any sense of what you saw, trust that your subconscious mind received the answers you requested. Then, as the situation unfolds, see if you can notice how the images applied. With practice, in time, you'll become much more comfortable interpreting the language of your subconscious mind.

Dream Interpretation Charm

If you wake up from a dream that feels significant to you but you can't seem to make heads or tails of it, try saying the following, adding each ingredient mentally as you do so. (To help someone else interpret a dream, speak each line and have him or her repeat it after you.)

> *My mind is a cauldron, and in the cauldron appears a dream.*
>
> *As I stir in a clockwise direction with a spoon*
> *of light, I add sunshine for illumination.*
>
> *I add moonlight for otherworld awareness.*
>
> *I add starlight for remembrance of interconnectedness.*
>
> *As above, so below; as within, so without.*
>
> *Diving into the cauldron, I follow the gossamer*
> *cords that interweave all to all.*
>
> *What do they tell me? With playfulness, I hazard a guess.*
>
> *If I had to make up a story about the meaning*
> *of this dream, what would it be?*

2: THE HOLISTIC ENERGY MAGIC SPELLBOOK

Now, without stopping or overthinking, answer your question through free writing or speaking aloud.

Dream Message Invocation

Because dreams are the language of the wise and sprawling subconscious, we can tap into them to glean solutions to problems that feel impossible for our conscious mind to solve or to gain confidence about decisions that our conscious mind is having trouble making. If you'd like to try this, say or think the following dream interpretation charm just after turning out the light and getting under the covers.

> As I swim into the ocean of starlight,
> I find the answers I seek.
> Upon awakening to the land of the sun,
> I retain them.

Then, as you wait for sleep to descend, go around and around in your mind, considering the issue or challenge from every angle. Literally exhaust your conscious mind until your sleeping mind takes over. Upon awakening, jot down or record everything you remember from your dream, even if it doesn't seem to make sense yet. Perform the dream interpretation charm again if necessary. Repeat nightly until you feel satisfied with what you've learned from your dreams.

Love Goddess Magic

The Goddess of Love is present in many cultures and is called by many names, including Venus, Aphrodite, Hathor, and Freya. And quite often she reigns over not just romantic love, but also charm, beauty, and attractiveness. The following spells fall under her romantic, mesmerizing, sensual domain.

Attract a Divine Partner

Working magic for attracting a partner must be done carefully. While of course we don't want to attract just anyone, I am not a proponent of the old "make a list of every quality you want in a partner" technique, as the Universe (or the part of us that is one with everything) knows much, much better than our rational mind what partner will be perfect for us at any given time. We're not ordering a pizza, after all; rather, we're attracting a multifaceted, complex human being with an ineffable eternal essence! With that in mind, in this ritual you'll begin by getting your vibration into a very clear and positive space because like attracts like, and then you'll set the clear intention to allow the Universe to find you a partner who is ideal for you in every way.

Oh, and never, never, *ever* do this or any spell to attract a partner while visualizing or naming a specific person, or prolonged misery for all concerned will certainly ensue. (Was that warning emphatic enough to dissuade you? I hope so! I like to think my egregious magical mistakes of the past were good for something!)

Wake up before sunrise on the morning of a new moon. Go outside and face east. Just as the sun peeks above the horizon, say:

> *I now invoke the power of the sunlight and the dawn.*
> *Please shine light in the dark spaces.*
> *Empower me, bless me, and steady me for love.*
> *Thank you.*

Feel the light of the sun blessing you with its gentle yet powerful energy.

The next morning, and every morning up until the morning of the full moon, as soon as you open your eyes in the morning (or at least sometime in the morning before you go about your day), feel sunlight shining on you and into your heart as you inwardly say:

> *Sun shines brightly into my heart.*
> *I am empowered, blessed, and ready for love.*

On the night of the full moon, go outside and gaze at the moon, basking in its gentle glow. Say:

Divine partner, I call to you now.

While I don't yet know your identity, the Universe sees you on my behalf and knows who you are.

Like the moon naturally attracts and receives the light of the sun, I invite you to come to me now.

You, divine partner, who I love and who loves me;
You, who I trust and who is trustworthy;
You, who are beautiful and who see me as beautiful;
You, who are perfect for me and for who I am perfect in all ways: obvious, subtle, expected, and unexpected;
I call you. I summon you. I invite you. I attract you.

Come to me.
Come to me.
Come to me.

Feel the receptive, mystical light of the moon bathing you and rendering you radiant and irresistibly magnetic. Note that you may attract a number of potential partners after this ritual: don't assume the first one that appears is the one. Instead, keep an open mind, honor the journey, and have fun!

Bless and Harmonize a Relationship

If you're in a romantic relationship, it goes without saying that you want to infuse it with the best and most auspicious possible vibes. Before you begin, cleanse yourself and your partner according to the instructions in the Cleansing and Clearing section. (Choose a personal cleanse and then do the "Cleanse for Another Person.") Then call on Aphrodite, the romance angels (a group of angels specifically suited to help with romantic intentions), or the Lord and Lady—whomever feels most powerful to you for this purpose—to bless your partnership with love, harmony, trust, and true intimacy. Feel/imagine/see them surrounding the two of you in a spiraling circle of pink light with gold sparkles. You can do this daily, weekly, or as needed.

You can also add bells and whistles to the visualization to make it more special or as the mood takes you. For example, you might imagine yourselves holding hands and standing in a soft rainfall of a clockwise whirlwind of pink and red rose petals. White rose petals moving in a counterclockwise direction, on the other hand, might be good for after an argument to heal and purify your relationship. At the conclusion of the ritual, you might imagine the romance angels placing flower crowns on your heads and kissing you each on the forehead to seal in the magic.

Create a Romantic Atmosphere

Whether or not you have the freedom to create a romantic ambience in the physical world, you can create the vibe in the nonphysical with this instant charm.

If you are able to set the stage for romance before any-one else is present in the space, spin in a clockwise direc-tion with your arms extended while you say the magic words below; otherwise, don't worry about it.

First, inwardly call on the Goddess of Love to bless your magical endeavor. Then imagine a circle of hovering candles (like floating candles, only in the air) around the perimeter of the space, appearing and lighting up in a clockwise direc-tion as you say (or think):

Beauty and love, illuminate! Thank you!

Now feel love and romance flowing out from your heart and filling the space. Know that everything within the circle of visualized candles will glow with beauty and significance, and that all romantic thoughts and feelings will be intensi-fied.

Heal a Relationship or a Broken Heart

If we are experiencing conflict or separation in a roman-tic relationship, we must remember that in the seemingly finite world in which we find ourselves, all romantic rela-tionships are simply not destined to be. However, in the true, eternal, transcendent world, we are one with every-thing and everyone. Our hearts are healed, and we can see ourselves and others as the miracles we are. In this ritual, we work on the transcendent plane so that we can allow Divine Source Energy to flow through our lives and relationships, leaving the most ideal and harmonious conditions in its wake. If an earthly relationship is for your truest good, it will be mended and continue on in the physical world. If it is not for your truest good, it will be mended in the nonphysical and released from the physical so that a relationship that *is* for your truest good can flow in.

Please note that for either eventuality, it is imperative that you let go of all grasping and attachment to outcome so that your romantic conditions can be characterized by non-codependent wholeness as well as trust in yourself, the other person, and the Divine.

Please also note that it's okay if you don't think the words exactly as they are written below. Just thinking words that have the same general meaning will work perfectly.

Sit or recline comfortably somewhere where you will not be disturbed. Be sure your spine is straight, and close your eyes. Allow your breath to deepen naturally. Notice where you are holding tension, and breathe into that tension as you allow it to release.

Now, in your mind's eye, journey to an interdimensional waterfall. It's a beautiful day. A fresh breeze is blowing white clouds across the sky, and the sun is shining brightly. All around the waterfall, healing herbs grow and lightly sway in the breeze: herbs like lemon balm, mint, lavender, and comfrey. This is the waterfall of healing. Still in your mind's eye, remove your clothes as a gesture of surrendering all attachment to outcome and trusting utterly in the Divine. Then step into the very clear, shallow pool. Feel the gravel under your feet as you approach and then stand under the rushing waterfall. Let the water cleanse you of any and all negativity or grasping related to your romantic relationship. As you stand under the cool, cleansing waterfall, think the words:

> *I now release all that is not love.*
>
> *I now release all that is not trust.*
>
> *I release attachment to form and outcome.*
>
> *I release the need to control or be controlled.*
>
> *I surrender completely to divine flow.*

When you feel sufficiently cleansed, exit the waterfall and recline on a large, warm, flat rock that borders or acts as an island within the stream. Feel the warm sun drying you and detoxifying you. Feel it completing you and restructuring your pattern so that you feel sufficiently nourished by your own love for yourself. See it surrounding you in a sphere of glowing healing light. As you recline here, think the words:

> *I am healthy and whole on my own.*
>
> *Love is infinite, and love is everywhere.*
>
> *I am in love with myself.*
>
> *I am in love with everyone.*
>
> *I am in love with life.*
>
> *I am love.*

When you feel happy and whole, in your mind's eye see the other person being cleansed under the waterfall. Know that although you are near, he or she can't see you. As you gaze at her, wish her well and release her fully so that the best situation can prevail without old hurts or harmful attachments. As you see her bathing in the waterfall, think these words:

> *I release you to the Divine.*
> *I release you to healing.*
> *I see you as beautiful.*
> *I see you as healed.*
> *I see you as whole.*
> *I wish you only well.*

Step off the rock and onto the green herbs growing by the side of the stream. Then see the other person emerge from the waterfall and bathe in the sunlight on the rock, just as you did before her. Send her love and surround her in a sphere of light. Think the words:

> *I release you with love,*
> *I release you with love,*
> *I release you with love.*

> *I trust that the best possible outcome and*
> *everyone's truest good will prevail.*

> *Thank you, thank you, thank you.*
> *Blessed be. And so it is.*

See the other person dissolve into light and disappear.

Revitalize a Romantic Relationship

Sometimes a solid relationship needs a pick-me-up: perhaps a little (or a lot) more romance, playfulness, or inti-
mate connection. In this case, it's pretty much always the
best policy—and ultimately the most effective tactic—to
cultivate and enhance the desired qualities within yourself.
Remember, after all, that the other person doesn't owe you
anything, and you are not dependent on him or her for your
happiness or romantic satisfaction. You are your own person
and the master of your own fate, just as he or she is.

So on a Friday, sit comfortably with your spine straight
and take some deep breaths, inhaling the imagined scent of
roses. Bathe yourself in very bright golden-pink light containing rose petals that move gently around you in a clockwise direction. Now call on the Goddess of Love in whatever
form feels the most powerful for you; you can call on Venus,
Aphrodite, Hathor, Freya, or simply the "Goddess of Love."

From the bottom of your heart, speak your truth. Explain
why you have called her and what you'd like her to help you
with in your relationship, always focusing on the qualities
and feelings you'd like to experience more of in your life
rather than the actions you'd like your partner to take.

Then request that she show you some ways that you can
begin to cultivate these feelings and qualities on your own.
Be open to any guidance you receive, which may appear in
the form of thoughts, images, and ideas. For example, you
might get the idea or receive an inner nudge to take a pole

dancing or belly dance class, take more sensual baths, or go on adventures and vacations on your own. Write down what you come up with. Then thank the goddess and see the light around you shrink while retaining its potency until it's a small sphere of light residing at the center of your heart. In the days and weeks to follow, act on your guidance. You'll be amazed at how your relationship changes as a result of the changes that you cultivate within yourself.

Beauty Glamour

The word *glamour* was originally used to describe a spell that changed or enhanced one's appearance in the eyes of another. Although this ritual does indeed change the way that you are seen, it doesn't work its magic on another, but rather on you. When you feel beautiful, you exude beauty, and that is, of course, what others will perceive. Something that makes this ritual especially lovely is that it promotes authenticity: it doesn't create the *illusion* of beauty but, in fact, brings out the real thing. (Because, after all, you are already beautiful beyond measure!) Perform it anytime you'd like to accentuate your unique beauty and infuse your presence with an air of authentic elegance and magnetism.

Close your eyes and feel that you are sitting or standing comfortably on a small island in the middle of an abundantly wide, shaded, rushing stream. Water flows over rocks and boulders, and a light breeze caresses the trees. Overhead, the sky is blue with pure white clouds drifting across the sky. The air feels perfect against your skin. As you stand in this beautiful landscape, let yourself drink in the beauty through your pores. Know that, just like nature herself, you are magnificently, splendidly gorgeous.

In your mind's eye, light a bundle of floral incense and hold it to the sky as it smokes.

Say:

> *Spirits of air, I honor you.*
> *Spirits of air, I summon you.*
> *See my beauty and bring it out.*
> *Cloak me in your finery.*

Begin to notice the sounds of birds singing around you. (Let them be any type of bird that appears in your mind or that feels right to you. They can be one species or several.) Although they aren't singing in a human language, you can sense that they are singing to you of your beauty. Feel appreciated, seen, and known by these magical winged creatures. As their song reaches a crescendo, they descend to the island and stand around you in a circle, admiring your gorgeousness as if you are a masterpiece in a museum. Then, in an instant, they all fly away, each leaving one or two feathers as tokens of appreciation for your beauty.

Say:

> *Spirits of air, I thank you!*

Before your eyes, these feathers now assemble themselves into a lovely boa that transforms into a vibrant, glittery color (let it be what it chooses to be) and wraps itself comfortably around your neck and shoulders. Notice that it's scented of

2: THE HOLISTIC ENERGY MAGIC SPELLBOOK

a delicious perfume or incense. Know that wherever you go for the rest of the day, the boa will be invisibly cloaking you, perfuming the air and trailing your irresistibly magnetic energy like the tail of a kite or a shooting star. Let the awareness of this luxurious, airy gift color your presence. Remember to periodically inhale its perfume and feel its feathery softness against your skin.

Turn On the Charm

Perhaps you're going to a party where you feel like being the belle of the ball, maybe you're meeting your partner's parents, or it could be that you've just been stopped for speeding. Whatever your reason for wanting to turn on the charm, this instant, two-part ritual has got you covered. The more often you do it, the easier and quicker it will become.

First, place yourself within your heart. Envision your heart like a huge picture window that's closed and has the shades drawn. Now see yourself throwing open the shades and raising the window of your heart to look out at a gorgeous, expansive meadow on a temperate summer day. It might make it more intense to conjure up the sounds of shades sliding and a window opening. Let your heart open and the breeze and the sunshine flow in. Notice creatures experiencing joy, and share that joy with them: perhaps you see fairies dancing, deer drinking from a stream, lovely maidens making daisy crowns, or children laughing and running barefoot through the grass.

Now, still inside your heart (with the fresh air in your lungs, sunlight on your face, and summer breeze caressing your skin), look down and notice a large lever with a bejeweled top sparkling in the sunlight and labeled *charm*. The lever may be all the way down or partially moved up. Now slide that lever *all the way* up. Return to your present moment awareness and feel that your entire being, starting with your heart, begins to glow more and more brightly, like a klieg light.

Heal Your Body Image

Contrary to popular propaganda designed to make us feel inadequate so that we will buy things, bodies of all shapes and sizes are beautiful. Unfortunately, for a lot of us, letting go of negative messages surrounding body image can be challenging, to say the least. But when you truly and unconditionally love your body—like you love, for example, a beloved child or animal companion—you think thoughts that heal it, eat food that nourishes it, and exercise in ways that benefit it, not to mention you just plain feel better.

This meditation will help support your efforts to see your body as the beautiful, wise, strong, divinely designed vessel of spirit that it is. Of course, if you have an eating disorder or other serious body image issue, it's important to get professional support.

While sitting comfortably with your spine straight, close your eyes, relax, and take some deep breaths. Really come into an awareness of your body: its weight on the cushion or ground, its temperature, and anything else that you may feel: aches, pains, or comfort. Now begin to notice your breath as it goes in and out: notice how your body feels when your lungs expand and how it feels when you breathe out through your nose or mouth. Continue to relax your body consciously as you inwardly recite *I breathe in relaxation* on the inhale and *I breathe out tension* on the exhale. Continue this while consciously relaxing your body until you feel deeply physically relaxed.

Then begin to inwardly recite *I breathe in approval* on the inhale and *I breathe out fear* on the exhale. As you do this, really choose to approve of yourself and your body in every way as you let go of any fears that you are in any way inadequate or not deserving of love. Feel in your body where you may have been holding onto these fears and really sigh them out right along with the breath.

When this feels complete, inwardly recite *I breathe in nourishment* on the inhale and *I breathe out fear* on the exhale. Now you're noticing that the breath nourishes and sustains you, and you're allowing every breath to be a gift and an act of love toward your body.

Next, inwardly recite *I breathe in love* on the inhale and *I breathe out fear* on the exhale. This time, feel completely loved and supported by the Universe and All That Is. Feel that you are surrounded by love, and let that love permeate every cell of your being as you continue to breathe out any lingering traces of fear of inadequacy or rejection.

Now, from this relaxed and attuned state, visualize/imagine/feel yourself as one with the earth—as nestled and cuddled in the lap of the Mother, who wants you to see yourself as she sees you: as the precious jewel you are. Stay with this feeling as you open yourself to any messages about how you can better express your loving devotion toward your body. For example, perhaps you'll realize that your body wants more fuzzy socks to wear around the house on chilly nights or that it wants to dance more often or drink less soda or eat more peaches.

Finish by thanking your body for this guidance and for all that it does for you all the time (like breathe, perceive, and propel you from place to place). And as an expression of your gratitude and your love, be sure to take action on your inner guidance today.

Success and Prosperity

Make a Way Where There Seemingly Is No Way

If you deeply desire to move forward in a certain area of your life, but you examine your mind and find within it the belief that it is impossible or highly improbable, banish this belief, open up to divine intervention, and make way for a miracle with the following ritual.

Close your eyes and inwardly invoke Ganesh with earnest words that convey something like the following:

> *Ganesh, I call on you! I know that you can make a way where there seemingly is no way. I know that you can clear the way for success and allow miracles to flow into my life experience. Please intervene now so that I may easily manifest the conditions I desire. Thank you!*

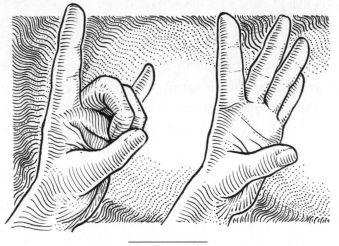

Expelling Mudra

Then perform the expelling mudra nine times. To do so, place your palms outward, elbows in against your sides, forearms angling up. Place your middle and ring fingers beneath your thumb tips and then flick them out forcefully. Each time you flick your fingers (again, nine times total—try counting in three sets of three), chant the words *Jai* (sounds like "jie") *Ganesha* (which means "glory, or victory, to Ganesh").

As you do so, feel that you are working with Ganesh to energetically remove obstacles and open doors. You might see doors opening in your mind's eye or simply feel confident that you are clearing negativity from your pathway.

Known and Seen Ritual

We are not all destined to be movie stars (nor would we all want to be), but when we are in alignment with our most ideal life path, we *are* destined to be known and seen in ways that bring joy to our hearts. We are a species that is hard-wired for connection, and there is no shame in wanting to be appreciated for our talents and strengths! Indeed, it is an important aspect of our nature. When this is expressed in an authentic way, it is an expression of our generosity—of wanting to share our gifts and our joy with others—rather than an expression of our ego.

With all of this in mind, if you'd like to be known and seen in the world for your unique abilities and strengths—perhaps to feel appreciated for your hard work or to gain desirable publicity for your business—try performing the following.

Call on the elements as outlined in chapter 2's simple daily alignment practice. Before releasing and thanking the elements, turn toward the south and tune in with the element of fire. Say:

> *Spirits of the South, ignite my flame.*
> *For my talents and strengths may I gain fame.*
>
> *Burning bright with vibrant fire,*
> *Make me one with my heart's desire.*
>
> *Like a shining, sparkling star,*
> *My light is seen from near and far.*
>
> *In my true authenticity,*
> *As I will, so mote it be.*

Feel yourself ignite like a giant candle flame standing above a wick that's grounded in your truest and most authentic depths. When this feels complete, thank and release the elements, starting with water (as in the simple daily alignment practice). Then return to the south and thank the fire element one last time from the bottom of your heart. Hold your hands over your heart to internalize the magic.

Lucky Dog

To summon luck into your life, conjure a tiny luck-drawing dog. After calling the elements and centering your mind, hold your hands about a foot and a half apart and envision a super cute little furry green dog hovering between them. Send love and divine light to the creature to breathe life into him or her. When the image of the hovering dog is clear in your mind, give him the name that seems to divinely fit him.

Explain that you'd like for him to go before you, creating lucky conditions and leading you in the direction of luck. Imbue him with the natural ability to know how to do this and to come back to you and whisper guidance in your ear. You may or may not hear or understand this guidance consciously, but trust that on a subtle (yet real) level, you will perceive it and respond to it. At least once per day (but perhaps more frequently) envision petting and sending love to the dog. Giving him treats and petting him in your mind's eye will keep his energetic signature strong.

Victory Is Mine

For victory in the form of literally winning a contest of some sort or in the form of simply achieving or following through in any endeavor or life area (such as writing a book or running a marathon), perform the following.

Please note that in the case of contests against others, this will not necessarily ensure your victory, as it won't interfere with the free will or the performance of your competitors; rather, it will help raise your performance to the most successful possible level that is in alignment with your truest good and the truest good of all.

Call the elements as instructed in the simple daily alignment practice. Then conjure up an image of a gold medal. See it hovering in the air. Mentally place it to the north and consecrate it with the element of earth by saying:

With earth, this medal is imbued
with strength and perseverance.

Mentally place it to the east and consecrate it with the element of air by saying:

With air, this medal is imbued
with freedom and ingenuity.

Place it to the south and consecrate it with fire by saying:

With fire, this medal is imbued
with passion and joy.

Place it to the west and consecrate it with water by saying:

> *With water, this medal is imbued*
> *with intuition and affluence.*

Place it above you and consecrate it with spirit by saying:

> *With spirit, this medal is imbued*
> *with the energy of divine victory.*

Now see the medal slip over your head. As you feel its magical energy merge with and activate your personal energy, say:

> *I am a winner and I deserve all good things.*
> *I am a magnet to victory.*
>
> *I am irresistibly drawn to victory, and*
> *victory is irresistibly drawn to me.*
>
> *I am surprised, again and again, in countless ways,*
> *by my amazing success and divine good fortune.*
>
> *Thank you, thank you, thank you.*
>
> *Blessed be. And so it is.*

Thank and release the elements.

Set the Stage for Success

If you're going somewhere to do something and you want it to be successful, perhaps try clearing the space and setting the energetic tone for success before you even arrive. For example, I try to remember to do this before my author events, but you could also do it before a job interview, an event you're hosting, or really anything else.

Once your mind is relaxed and centered, call to mind or connect with the space in which you'd like to experience success. If you've never been there before, you can think of the address or the name of the venue, or even just think of "the location where the event will take place." The important thing is being confident that you have the ability to connect with the energy of the space—and you do!

Once you've made contact, ask archangel Michael to powerfully vacuum and clear the energy of the space. Ask him to remove any and all stuck energy, negativity, earthbound spirits, or anything else that is less than ideal. Visualize or feel him doing this. Then, inwardly or aloud, thank him.

Next, ask Saint Germain to purify the space with his violet flame (see or sense him sending it throughout the space, transmuting any negativity into positivity and love) and then fine-tune the energy of the space to exactly the frequency that will best support your success. You may see or sense him doing this by sending an auditory tone or a geometrical pattern through the space, but simply asking him is all you need to do. Be sure to thank him when he's finished.

Finally, request that a circle of angels surround the space, preserving and protecting this vibration so that it will be just as clear and positive when you arrive. And then, of course, thank them too!

Legal Success

If you find yourself in a court battle or sticky legal situation, *and you are entirely in the right,* call on Forseti, the Norse god of justice. When you feel his presence arrive like a swift, loving, and intimidating (to those who would do you harm) father figure, express the emotion of gratitude and direct it toward him. From a feeling place, send him love and reverence in the form of bright light in order to nourish his etheric presence in your consciousness and in the world.

Then, with or without words, show him the situation. Because he speaks the language of emotion and symbol, you might picture the whole thing as if you're picturing the storyline and emotions of a movie. Be sure to feel your feelings and project them to him as well. Imagine that you are illuminating the dark spaces and shining light on the true situation. Once you feel that you've conveyed the situation as thoroughly as possible, ask Forseti to intervene on your behalf and bring you the justice that you deserve.

Say:

> *Forseti, the presiding one,*
> *Please stay with me till this thing's done.*

Bring justice from your golden hall
Swiftly and once and for all.

I honor you with love and light
And thank you for your wisdom bright!

Throughout your legal proceedings, know that Forseti is with you, intervening powerfully on your behalf. Remember to thank him again after justice has been served.

Joy Gifting Spree

To open your heart, open doors to abundance and luck, and generally put you in an awesome mood, go on a joy gifting spree. Close your eyes and picture someone you really love. Then give them all the stuff or put them in all the situations that would make them the most joyful. In your mind's eye, see them laughing and smiling.

As time permits, repeat with other people: people you love, people you like, people you don't like, and people you kind of know. If you don't know what would make someone joyful, just pretend that you do. Always finish with yourself.

Whirlwind of Gratitude

You can do this one anywhere and anytime: for example, while you're waiting in line, driving your car, or reclining at home. It's an instant mood brightener and energy booster—and an added bonus is that it gets you into an abundant mindset, which automatically magnetizes prosperity and luck. It works according to the law of attraction and its oft-repeated mantra that *what you focus on expands*.

Simply begin to marvel at all your many blessings while inwardly saying *Thank you for [everything you can think of]*. For example, your inner monologue might go something like this:

"Thank you for the sky. Thank you for clean water to drink. Thank you for my husband. Thank you for electricity. Thank you for the money that I have in the bank. Thank you for music. Thank you for my beating heart. Thank you for my legs. Thank you for cookies. Thank you for cats. Thank you for clouds. Thank you for flowers (and so on)."

As you do this, imagine all this wonderful, prosperous energy being activated and beginning to swirl around you in a clockwise direction, constantly gaining momentum and power.

Lakshmi Wealth Activation

If your finances could use a quick pick-me-up or if you just feel like magically drawing more wealth into your life, perform the following. It's best if it's done when the moon is between new and full, but in a pinch it can be done anytime.

While sitting or standing with your spine straight, close your eyes and hold your palms up to the sky with your elbows in against your sides and your forearms angling up, as if you are holding a platter out in front of you at heart level. Consciously relax your body and center your mind as you focus your attention at your third eye and breathe in and out in a relaxed way. Inwardly or aloud, call on Lakshmi, the beautiful Hindu goddess of wealth (aka Mahalakshmi) by saying:

Mahalakshmi, Mahalakshmi, Mahalakshmi.

Then imagine her presence arriving with the sound of clear rushing water and abundant tinkling coins. You might also conjure up the scent of fresh jasmine. Feel her pouring golden, sparkly, coin-filled light into each of your open palms. As she does this, know that she is literally blessing you with the energy of affluence. Know in your heart that you are already wealthy at this very moment. Then say to Lakshmi:

Thank you! Thank you! Thank you!

Feel this golden, affluent, jasmine-scented, coin-filled light surrounding you and cocooning you in a clockwise swirl of movement. Open your eyes and know that because of the metaphysical law that states that like attracts like (also known as "the rich get richer"), the fact that you have been divinely blessed with affluent energy will draw physical affluence into your life, effective immediately.

Open the Door to Wealth

If you're really working on expanding your finances and your prosperity consciousness, try this extremely simple ritual once per day for an entire moon cycle, starting at the new moon. Alternatively, you might do it at the new or full moon, every time you clean house, or really anytime you feel like it.

Open your front door. Standing at the threshold, facing out, say or think these words:

> *I now open the door to wealth.*
>
> *I invite blessings, luxury, and abundance.*
>
> *Welcome! Welcome! Welcome!*

Magic to the Rescue

Retrieving Lost Objects

Divine Mind Invocation

If you seem to have lost something important and you want to retrieve it, stop what you're doing, close your eyes, and relax. Take at least three deep breaths and then remind yourself that while you're temporarily having a finite human life, in actuality you are one with the Infinite: you are one with the Divine. Feel your consciousness as it expands out of your little body and embraces and touches All That Is. This is your true mind. Now say to yourself with great conviction:

Nothing is lost in Divine Mind.
Nothing is lost in Divine Mind.
Nothing is lost in Divine Mind.

Feel your Infinite consciousness locating the object and bringing it back into contact with your physical body. Feel confident in the ability of your omniscient divine self to reunite you with the object. Open your eyes.

Golden Net Visualization

If something important appears to be irretrievably lost, stop your negative thought process and reformulate it with the following visualization.

Close your eyes, take some deep breaths, and relax. Now send your consciousness into the cosmos and locate a cache of cosmic, golden light. Bring this light down into the atmosphere and create a thoughtform in the sky of a gigantic, earth-sized golden net. Charge this net with the intention to move through everything like a knife through butter except for the item that you are missing. Charge it with the intention to capture the item that you are missing and to deliver it straight back into your personal vicinity. Now visualize this net moving through the entire planet, knowing that it will not fail to gather the object and bring it to you, wherever it may be.

Irresistible Magnet Charm

This magnet charm was inspired by a similar "find it" spell once taught to me by my dear friend, the author Ellen Dugan, when I left my Kindle on a plane. Close your eyes, relax, and bring to mind the item that you seem to have lost. See it as clearly as possible from every angle. Now charge it with powerful magnetic energy. Hold your open palms up in front of you and charge them with powerful magnetic energy that irresistibly draws the item back into your possession.

As you keep this feeling and visualization in your hands and mind, say or think:

> *My hands are magnets and wherever you are*
> *You now return from near or far.*

Imagine actually magnetizing the item. Catch it in your hands and feel certain that it is already back in your possession. Open your eyes. Whenever the object comes to mind, release any fear and feel confident that it's on its way back to you now.

Invisibility and Concealment

Please note: as with any invisibility ritual or spell, you must also behave as inconspicuously as possible. These rituals will help conceal you but are not foolproof in and of themselves.

Black Velvet Concealment Charm

To render yourself as invisible as possible at a moment's notice or to conceal your thoughts, motives, or behaviors, in your mind's eye wrap yourself in a generous sheet of absorbent black velvet while also imagining that you can magically see through this velvet. As you're doing this, inwardly chant *black velvet* over and over again.

Blend into a Crowd

If you're in a crowd and you don't want another person or group of people in that crowd to spot you and single you out, feel and envision that you are not your individual self but rather the entire faceless, identity-less crowd. To intensify and magnify this visualization, rephrase Walt Whitman's line "out of the rolling ocean the crowd" and reverse its meaning as you inwardly chant:

I am the rolling ocean, the crowd
I am the rolling ocean, the crowd
I am the rolling ocean, the crowd.

Continue chanting this for as long as you need to stay inconspicuous.

Mirrored Sphere Visualization

To immediately conceal yourself, visualize a sphere of mirrors surrounding you like a giant bubble. While eyes may still be drawn in your direction, they will be drawn because of the movement of energy or the light bouncing off the mirrors, and therefore they will not be as likely to see you but rather other things or themselves. I like to do this when I feel self-conscious or overly sensitive and would simply prefer not to be seen. An added benefit is that it protects you from the negative thoughts and energy of others.

Miscellaneous

Deal with a Challenging Person

Between coworkers, business acquaintances, neighbors, community members, family, and extended family, there may be a time when you find it necessary to regularly interact with someone whom you would much prefer lived on another planet. As an extremely social species that feel best when we're harmoniously connecting with our fellow humans, a challenging relationship like this just may be one of the prickliest and most harrowing situations we find it necessary to experience.

Having had some experience in this area, I have learned quite well that I am not an expert, and I suspect that very few people are. Nevertheless, I am often asked about how to deal with challenging people, and while I can't provide a neat solution to every such predicament, I can offer a ritual that may offer some support. First, though, since you'll want to adopt the most advantageous perspective, let's look at some helpful things to keep in mind.

When I'm stuck in traffic, I have found that everything flows more smoothly when I stop the inner fight against it and embrace it to the best of my ability. Fighting it is not going to make it go faster anyway, and it's only going to create more stress, which carries all sorts of physical and emotional problems in its wake. Not to mention, when I honestly surrender and enjoy the extra time in my car, I swear the traffic starts to move faster. Similarly, if you absolutely have to interrelate with a certain person for some really valid reason—if there's nothing you can reasonably do to cease interacting with this person altogether—it's not going to do you any good to rail against this reality, and it may even do you some harm.

Let's be clear: I'm not saying that you shouldn't speak your truth with love when necessary. You totally, totally should. I'm saying that when you begin by accepting the situation fully and with as much gratitude and equanimity as possible, whatever truth you speak or action you take is much more likely to be effective and agreeable for all concerned. Not to mention, you'll be instantly saving yourself from the most challenging aspect of the relationship: namely, the stress.

If you can't think of a way to feel gratitude for someone with whom you have so many challenges, consider these words from the Dalai Lama:

> When we are faced with an enemy, a person or group of people wishing us harm, we can view this as an opportunity to develop patience and tolerance. We need these qualities: they are useful to us. And the only occasion we have to develop them is when we are challenged by an enemy. So, from this point of view...enemies are very beneficial, a blessing.

Now, this all sounds well and good on paper, but when we're in the thick of things it's not always so easy. Especially because life sometimes likes to give us situations that are precisely what we feel we have the least ability to accept, purposely designed that way because we need exactly that sort of kick in the pants in order to grow spiritually in the way our soul most wants to grow. So don't beat yourself up if you can't be the Dalai Lama about it right away. Just do your very best to stand up for yourself as necessary while also embracing the situation like it's a gift to you from the Universe. (Because, after all, your very best is all you can ever do.)

Now that you have the proper mindset in place, you'll want to begin by casting a circle by facing each cardinal direction and calling on the five elements (earth, air, water, fire, and spirit) as you learned to do in chapter 2. Sit in your circle and relax, deeply connecting with the Divine in a way that feels powerful for you. Visualize yourself in a sphere of divine light and know that you are completely connected and tuned into all wisdom and love.

Hold up your hands so that your palms are facing up, elbows slightly raised away from your body, as if holding a large serving platter. Then conjure up the challenge in your body and mind. You might see the person's face in your mind or feel the anger or frustration in your body. You might also explain your challenge to the Universe as you would explain a disagreement with a playmate to a teacher or parental figure as a child. As you do this, visualize offering this challenge as energy that you are offering up to the Divine. See this challenging energy forming as a large sphere that you're holding in your hands like a giant beach ball. Don't censor or whitewash your feelings at this point; just get it all up and out, through your palms and into the sphere.

Inwardly or aloud, explain to the Divine (or the part of you that is one with All That Is) that you don't know what to do in this situation but that you know the Divine knows exactly what to do. Explain that you want to behave with the utmost integrity, that you want to be fair to yourself and others, and that you desire the best possible outcome for everyone involved. Also explain that you're willingly releasing this challenge and offering it up to the Divine for perfect healing, purification, and transmutation.

Once you make this declaration, feel that the sphere is becoming lighter and lighter, moving up and into the divine wisdom like a soap bubble rising into the sky. Really allow yourself to release all the tension, worry, fear, and stress surrounding the situation, and trust that (with divine help) you'll know exactly what you need to know and exactly what you need to do.

As you see the sphere move upward and dissolve into the light, know that you've successfully handed your challenge off to the Divine, and express gratitude from the depths of your heart. Thank the elements, and open the circle.

Stop a Challenging Mental Pattern

If your thinking ever gets into an almost unbearable rut, you might try this: choose to like the mental pattern and pretend as if you want it to be exactly as it is. This often works because fighting against it is often the thing that perpetuates it.

For example, sometimes I feel uncomfortable in certain social situations. During those times, it always passes the most quickly when I stop fighting against it and instead get my inner thought pattern go something like, "Oh good, I get to feel this shyness again. Now I can have so much sympathy and understanding when other people feel shy. Now I can really understand the concept of shy on a deep level if I ever get asked about it during a workshop," etc. If you can find some way to begin to embrace the mental pattern, the tension around it will disperse and it will often dissolve in the light of acceptance.

Nightmare Transmutation Charm

When you have a nightmare, instead of banishing it or stuffing it down, embrace it and reclaim the energy that has been co-opted by your fear. This little charm will help.

With your elbows in against your sides, angle your forearms up, palms facing out, and touch your little and ring finger tips to your thumb tip, with your index and middle fingers extended. (This is called "prana mudra.")

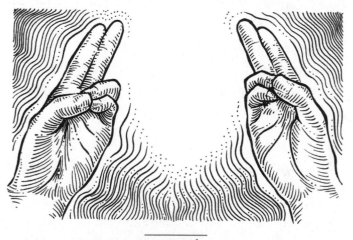

Prana Mudra

Take three deep breaths through your nose, breathing out through puckered lips. Then say:

This dream is a wild mare that has run to me
In the night, and I listen to its teaching.

I feel the fear, and now it changes into love.

I feel the love, and that love is also strength.

I feel the strength, and that strength is also power.

I feel the power as a bright and glorious surge,
And I give thanks for the wisdom of the mare.

With hands still in prana mudra, finish up with three more breaths in through the nose and out through puckered lips.

For frequent or recurring nightmares, do this faithfully until they effectively change or subside. To gain more insight, you might follow up with the dream interpretation charm as desired.

Clap Your Way Out of a Funk

Like a long song improvised by expert musicians during a jam session, we are each a unique pattern of energy that makes itself up as it goes along. Also like a long song improvised during a jam session, we can sometimes get stuck in boring ruts that require a fresh burst of movement and change. This ritual will help precipitate just such a positive energetic shift. In the days and weeks after you perform it, you will be alert to new possibilities and generally feel that positivity is more apparent and available in your life experience.

Move through each room and area of your home in a counterclockwise direction while clapping loudly. As you clap, feel that you are clearing stagnant energy, breaking apart old patterns, and getting things moving in a positive way. Stand in a central location and rotate in a counterclockwise circle as you continue to clap loudly. As you do so, feel that you are clearing and activating your personal energy.

Then begin clapping more lightly and quickly as you raise your hands up and clap to the sky. Then place them down near the floor and clap to the floor. Clap to your left and to your right. Move your hands back to a comfortable position in front of you as you continue to clap more and more rapidly, feeling that you are getting stuck and slow energy moving at a quicker and healthier rate.

When this feels like it reaches a crescendo, fling your hands up in the air as if you're throwing petals to the sky. Then place your right hand on your heart and your left hand on your belly. Feel the pulse and flow of the clean, fresh energy that you've set in motion. Smile.

Conclusion

You are a precious and unique channel of All That Is. When you align with and manifest your most authentic desires, rest assured that your happiness and success bring great benefits to the web of life and to all beings in all directions of time. Let us each remember to live our greatness and express our vast personal power with humility and with the clear intention to bring peace and healing to all.

Acknowledgments

I would like to thank Rebecca Zins, Elysia Gallo, Bill Krause, Sandra Weschcke, Kat Sanborn, Anna Levine, Katie Mickschl, and everyone at Llewellyn. I would also like to thank my boyfriend, Ted Bruner, and my dear friends and magical support system: Ellen Dugan, Rachel Avalon, Angela Taylor, Janine Jordan, and Sedona Ruiz.

This book is dedicated to the memory of Acorn, whose adorable face and huge green eyes I so look forward to seeing again one day on the other side.

Bibliography

Andrews, Ted. *How to Heal with Color*. St. Paul, MN: Llewellyn, 2001.

Brett, Ana, and Ravi Singh. *A Journey Through the Chakras* (DVD). New York: Raviana.com, 2005.

Brown, Brene. *Daring Greatly: How the Courage to Be Vulnerable Transforms the Way We Live, Love, Parent, and Lead*. New York: Gotham Books, 2012.

Carroll, Cain, and Revital Carroll. *Mudras of India: A Comprehensive Guide to the Hand Gestures of Yoga and Indian Dance*. London: Singing Dragon, 2012.

Chevalier, Gaétan, et. al. "Earthing: Health Implications of Reconnecting the Human Body to the Earth's Surface Electrons," *Journal of Environmental and Public Health*. January 2012, http://dx.doi.org/10.1155/2012/291541.

Collins, Terah Kathryn. *The Western Guide to Feng Shui*. Carlsbad, CA: Hay House, 1996.

"Comte de Saint-Germain," *Encyclopedia Britanica.* 2013, http://www.britannica.com/EBchecked/ topic/517187/comte-de-Saint-Germain.

Cooper, Diana, and Kathy Crosswell. *Ascension Through Orbs.* Findhorn, Scotland: Findhorn Press, 2009.

Cunningham, Scott. *Cunningham's Encyclopedia of Magical Herbs.* St. Paul, MN: Llewellyn, 1985.

———. *Magical Aromatherapy: The Power of Scent.* St. Paul, MN: Llewellyn, 1989.

Dalai Lama. *An Open Heart: Practicing Compassion in Everyday Life.* New York: Little, Brown, 2001.

Dugan, Ellen, and Mark Evans. *Witches Tarot.* Woodbury, MN: Llewellyn, 2012.

Dugan, Ellen. *Practical Protection Magick: Guarding and Reclaiming Your Power.* Woodbury, MN: Llewellyn, 2011.

Eckstut, Arielle, and Joann Eckstut. *The Secret Language of Color: Science, Nature, History, Culture, Beauty of Red, Orange, Yellow, Green, Blue & Violet.* New York: Black Dog and Leventhal, 2013.

Elliott, Carolyn. *Awesome Your Life: The Artist's Antidote to Suffering Genius.* Ninety-Nine (Per)cent Press, 2011.

Embre, Lester, and Thomas Nenon, ed. *Phenomenology 2005, 5: Selected Essays from North America, Part 2.* Zeta Books, 2007.

Fincham, Johnny. *The Spellbinding Power of Palmistry: New Insights into an Ancient Art.* Long Barn, England: Green Magic, 2005.

Haner, Jean. *The Wisdom of Your Face: Change Your Life with Chinese Face Reading!* Carlsbad, CA: Hay House, 2008.

Hicks, Esther, and Jerry Hicks. *Ask and It Is Given: Learning to Manifest Your Desires.* Carlsbad, CA: Hay House, 2004.

Howell, L. Daniel. *The Barefoot Book: 50 Great Reasons to Kick off Your Shoes.* Alameda, CA: Hunter House, 2010.

Illes, Judika. *Element Encyclopedia of 5000 Spells: The Ultimate Reference Book for the Magical Arts.* London: HarperElement, 2004.

———. *Encyclopedia of Mystics, Saints, and Sages: A Guide to Asking for Protection, Wealth, Happiness, and Everything Else!* New York: HarperCollins, 2011.

———. *Encyclopedia of Spirits: The Ultimate Guide to the Magic of Fairies, Genies, Demons, Ghosts, Gods, and Goddesses.* New York: HarperCollins, 2009.

"Inspiration." Merriam-Webster.com, 2014. www.merriam-webster.com.

Kennedy, David Daniel. *Feng Shui for Dummies.* Hoboken, NJ: Wiley Publishing, 2001.

Lau, Theodora. *The Handbook of Chinese Horoscopes*, sixth ed. New York: HarperCollins, 2007.

Linn, Denise. *Past Lives and Beyond* (digitally remastered audio). QED Productions, 2007.

Manning, Al G. *Helping Yourself with White Witchcraft*. West Nyak, NY: Parker Publishing, 1972.

Marquis, Melanie. *The Witch's Bag of Tricks: Personalize Your Magick and Kickstart Your Craft*. Woodbury, MN: Llewellyn, 2011.

———. *The Witch's World of Magick: Expanding Your Practice with Techniques & Traditions from Diverse Cultures*. Woodbury, MN: Llewellyn, 2014.

Melody. *Love Is in the Earth: A Kaleidoscope of Crystals*. Wheat Ridge, CO: Earth Love Publishing House, 1995.

Penczak, Christopher. *Ascension Magick: Ritual, Myth & Healing for the New Aeon*. Woodbury, MN: Llewellyn, 2008.

Pierson, PJ, and Mary Shipley. *Aromatherapy for Everyone: Discover the Scents of Health and Happiness with Essential Oils*. Garden City Park, NY: Square One, 2004.

Prophet, Elizabeth Clare. *Saint Germain: Master Alchemist*. Gardiner, MT: Summit University Press, 2004.

———. *Violet Flame to Heal Body, Mind & Soul*. Gardiner, MT: Summit University Press, 1997.

Rinpoche, Tsoknyi. *Open Heart, Open Mind: Awakening the Power of Essence Love.* New York: Harmony, 2012.

Sage, Angie. *Septimus Heap, Book One: Magyk.* New York: Harper Trophy, 2005.

Shinn, Florence Scovel. *The Wisdom of Florence Scovel Shinn.* New York: Fireside, 1989.

Tolle, Eckhart. *The Power of Now: A Guide to Spiritual Enlightenment.* Novato, CA: New World Library, 1999.

Venolia, Carol. *Healing Environments: Your Guide to Indoor Well-Being.* Celestial Arts, 1988.

Virtue, Doreen, and Lynette Brown. *Angel Numbers: The Angels Explain the Meaning of 111, 444, and Other Numbers in Your Life.* Carlsbad, CA: Hay House, 2005.

Virtue, Doreen. *Angel Therapy: Healing Messages for Every Area of Your Life.* Carlsbad, CA: Hay House, 1997.

———. *Archangels and Ascended Masters: A Guide to Working and Healing with Divinities and Deities.* Carlsbad, CA: Hay House, 2003.

———. *Archangels and Ascended Masters Oracle Cards.* Carlsbad, CA: Hay House, 2007.

———. *Goddess Guidance Oracle Cards.* Carlsbad, CA: Hay House, 2004.

Webster, Richard. *Face Reading Quick and Easy.* Woodbury, MN: Llewellyn, 2012.

Whitefeather, Sapokaneona. *Master Meditations.* Spirit Hawk Recordings, 2004.

Whitehurst, Tess. *The Good Energy Book: Creating Harmony and Balance for Yourself and Your Home.* Woodbury, MN: Llewellyn, 2012.

———. *The Magic of Flowers: A Guide to Their Metaphysical Uses and Properties.* Woodbury, MN: Llewellyn, 2013.

———. *Magical Fashionista: Dress for the Life You Want.* Woodbury, MN: Llewellyn, 2013.

Whitman, Walt. *Leaves of Grass.* New York: Mentor, 1954.

Wolfe, Amber. *Personal Alchemy: A Handbook of Healing and Self-Transformation.* St. Paul, MN: Llewellyn, 1995.

Woolfolk, Joanna Martine. *The Only Astrology Book You'll Ever Need: New Edition.* Lanham, Maryland: Madison Books, 2001.

Yun, Lin, and Sarah Rossbach. *Living Color: Master Lin Yun's Guide to Feng Shui and the Art of Color.* New York: Kodansha America, 1994.

Index

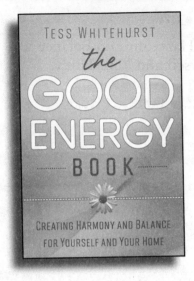

TESS WHITEHURST

the

GOOD ENERGY BOOK

BOOK

CREATING HARMONY AND BALANCE
FOR YOURSELF AND YOUR HOME

The Good Energy Book
Creating Harmony and Balance for Yourself and Your Home

Tess Whitehurst

This gem of a book teaches you how to become a fountain of good energy. Discover how to maintain positive energy in your home and establish lifelong habits and perspectives that will bring happiness and attract all good things.

Popular author and columnist Tess Whitehurst presents a holistic system for keeping your energy positive and traversing any place, situation, or challenge with confidence, clarity, and grace. She shares fun and effective techniques that draw from both the physical and energetic realms, telling you not just what to do, but also why you're doing it and even how it works.

978-0-7387-2772-1 • 5³⁄₁₆ x 8 • 264 pages

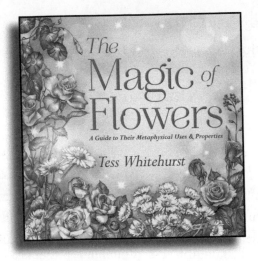

The
Magic of
Flowers

A Guide to Their Metaphysical Uses & Properties

Tess Whitehurst

The Magic of Flowers
A Guide to Their Metaphysical Uses & Properties

Tess Whitehurst

From African daisy to ylang-ylang and seventy-six others in between, Tess Whitehurst's *The Magic of Flowers* introduces you to the holistic and healing benefits of the most magical flowers, flower essences, floral essential oils, and more. This one-of-a-kind, comprehensive, and convenient guide explores the subtle and whimsical realm of flower magic.

As a manifestation of divine beauty and wisdom, each flower offers you unique magical and spiritual ways to connect with it. Enjoy healing, spiritual growth, and the life conditions you desire by using flowers for aromatherapy, charms and rituals, herbal potions, divine alignment, and more. If you've always wanted to commune with flowers in holistic ways, this is the book for you.

978-0-7387-3194-0 • 7½ x 7½ • 432 pages

To Write to the Author

If you wish to contact the author or would like more information about this book, please write to the author in care of Llewellyn Worldwide and we will forward your request. Both the author and the publisher appreciate hearing from you and learning of your enjoyment of this book and how it has helped you. Llewellyn Worldwide cannot guarantee that every letter written to the author can be answered, but all will be forwarded. Please write to:

Tess Whitehurst
c/o Llewellyn Worldwide
2143 Wooddale Drive
Woodbury, MN 55125-2989

Please enclose a self-addressed stamped envelope for reply
or $1.00 to cover costs. If outside the USA, enclose an
international postal reply coupon.

Many of Llewellyn's authors have websites with additional information and resources. For more information, please visit our website:

WWW.LLEWELLYN.COM

31901056301726

Magic  here

You are a magical _____ create positive change and manife_____ ____rweaving both ancient and modern spiritual techniques in a uniquely accessible way, this book will help you transform your personal challenges into beautiful opportunities for growth, expansion, and new understanding.

Holistic Energy Magic provides instructions for tool-free magic and important insights into the foundations of personal power: intention, visualization, symbolic action, grateful expectation, and alignment with All That Is. In this exceptionally empowering book, you'll learn how to:

- Cultivate and deepen your relationship with the five elements
- Develop your invisible magical toolbox
- Create an energetic palette of color, light, crystals, flowers, and sounds
- Develop working relationships with angels, ancestors, animals, and other allies
- Interpret symbols and dreams for a deeper alignment with All That Is

Complete with a spellbook of charms and invocations for protection, serenity, love, and prosperity, this book shares the precious secrets of attuning your life to the frequency of your truest and most authentic desires.

Ted Bruner

TESS WHITEHURST is an intuitive counselor, energy worker, feng shui consultant, and speaker. The award-winning author of *Magical Housekeeping*, *The Magic of Flowers*, and *The Good Energy Book*, Tess has appeared on the Bravo show *Flipping Out* and her articles have appeared in *Writer's Digest* and *Whole Life Times*. Tess lives in Columbia, Missou~~~ ~~~~~ ~~~~ ~~~ ~~ ~~~~~~~~~~~~~~~~ ~~~

$16.99

ISBN 978

9 780738 745374

LLEWELLYN

www.llewellyn.com • Facebook.com/LlewellynBooks • Twitter:@LlewellynBooks